D1153298

Handles

Handles for different pieces of pottery can be made by either "pulling" or "extruding" techniques, depending on your personal preference and the style of the pottery you are making.

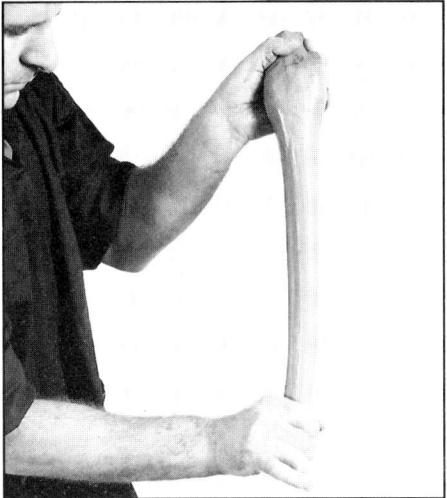

Pulling a handle

1 Pat a large lump of well-prepared clay into a thick carrot shape. Hold the clay comfortably, slim end pointing down. Lubricate your hands and the clay thoroughly and begin to tease the clay down, stretching it with a rhythmic action. Be careful not to increase the pressure applied at any point since this will cause weakness in the handle.

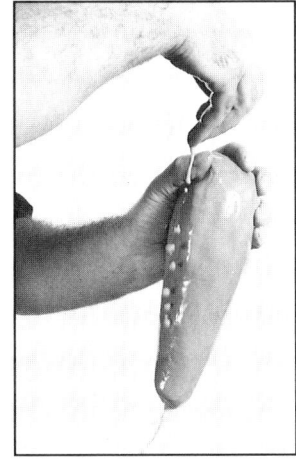

2 As you pull keep twisting your wrist through 180° to ensure that the handle develops evenly. As the handle thins out, alter its shape by changing the position of the fingers of your right hand. Flatten your thumb towards the palm of your hand to form a narrow U-shape.

3 Running your hand down the handle in this position will develop a flattened shape. When the handle has thinned down to the correct width to suit the piece for which you have pulled it, run your thumb firmly down the centre to make a shallow groove. The length and thickness of the handle is determined by the object it is to fit, but the principle remains the same no matter what size the handle is to be. Once you are happy that you have pulled enough clay for however many handles you need, divide it up and leave the strips to stiffen slightly before attaching them. You can shape the handles when the clay is still pliable enough to create the sort of shape that you require.

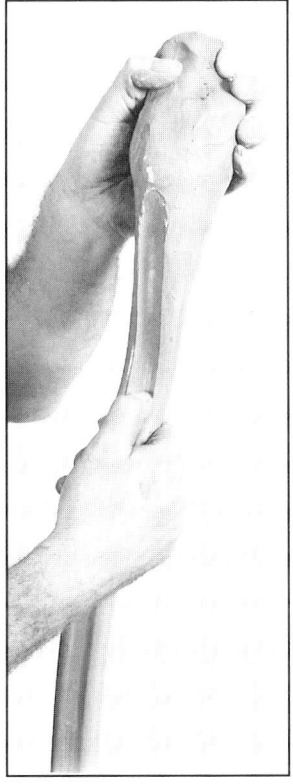

Extruding a handle

Handles can be made very quickly by extruding from a pugmill or extruder. Die plates designed for this purpose can be bought, or made by carefully cutting out a template from a suitable sheet of metal. You can extrude a handle from a block of soft clay with a piece of stiff wire. Bend the wire with pliers to form the sectional shape you need for a handle. Draw the wire, held vertically, through the top layer to the length of the handle you need. The wire will slice through the clay, extruding a shaped segment of clay as it passes through.

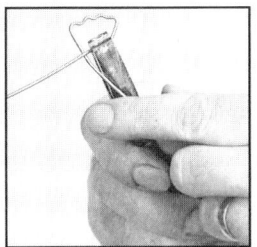

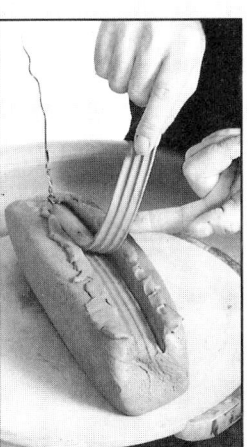

Working with large pieces of clay

Centring

1 Use very well-prepared clay when throwing large forms. Pat the lump of clay into an even, rounded dome to make centring easier. Keep the wheel at a steady rate, slower than that needed to centre smaller pieces of clay. Begin to move the off-centred clay up to the top. The effort required to centre a large piece is not that much greater than that required for a small amount, but it is tiring. Begin to cone the clay. ▷

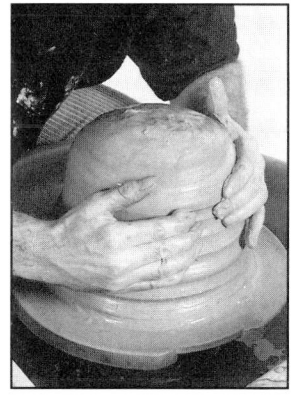

The sheer exhilaration involved in handling large amounts of clay successfully on the wheel makes this aspect of throwing particularly appealing to most potters. Few enthusiasts can resist the challenge presented to them by large pieces of clay, and a successful end result can promote an enormous sense of achievement.

Even beginners can expect to progress fairly rapidly as they learn to handle large amounts of clay. Any problems are usually the result of a generally poor throwing technique rather than any intrinsic difficulties. A poor technique can often be disguised when throwing small pieces, because structural weaknesses are less noticeable; the opposite is true when throwing large pieces – any shortcomings or mistakes are highlighted and substantially exaggerated.

2 As you push the cone down, keep one elbow braced on the wheel tray and the other tucked into your side. Spend a while centring before you open the clay by pushing your thumb into it. If necessary, use your fist to force the clay to open. Slow the wheel down. △

3 Gripping your hands together begin to form the base and lift the walls. Maintain pressure between your hands and a steadying support as the walls extend. Keep the clay well lubricated, but do not allow it to build up in the base. ▷

Composite forms

Large forms can also be made by assembling several small thrown pieces. These composite forms can be made to a more complex design than a "thrown-in-one" pot, and the method employed is very simple. Each thrown section should be left to stiffen slightly before they are assembled. You must also ensure that the diameters of the rims to be joined together are equal and that the walls of all the forms are equally thick, to avoid uneven shrinkage and cracking at the joint. Centre one section at a time, score its rim, apply slurry and join the next piece.

Throwing coiled additions

The size of the forms you make need only determined by the size of the kiln you have at your disposal. A succession of sections can be added to a slightly stiffened form, thrown, allowed in turn to stiffen and be added to. These extra sections can be added as coils, freshly thrown pieces, or stiffened pieces with a throwable top section.

1 Throw a sturdy base section from the greatest weight you can manage with a levelled, thickened rim and leave it until it has stiffened slightly. Roll a thick, even coil of clay and attach it with slurry to the scored rim of the base section, compressing it into a squared roll. ▷

2 Take particular care to seal the join between the ends of the coil, because this can be a particularly weak area in the clay wall. Smooth the edge of the clay coil down over the rim with your thumb. Leave the coil in place to settle before you begin to throw. Lubricate the clay and begin to throw in the usual way. ▷

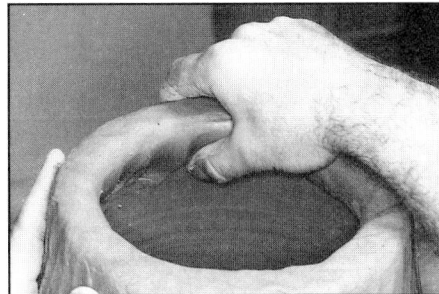

3 Concentrate on the top of the base section and the new coil where the clay is most receptive to alteration. Trim the rim and allow this new form to stiffen before repeating the process, should you wish to. △

Combining the Techniques

Throw a sturdy base section on a removable wheel bat. Measure its rim diameter and leave it to stiffen. Do not cut it free with a cutting wire. Throw a second section in the same way with an equal rim diameter and a thickened base. Leave this on the wheel bat to stiffen. Score both rims and re-locate the first form in the wheel. Apply slurry to its rim and attach the inverted second form to it, holding the wheel bat as you do so. Check that the two rims are aligned and smooth the join over. Remove the wheel bat from the top. Cut a hole in the thick base of the inverted form, just large enough for you to insert your hand and throw from the band of clay around the rim of the pot.

Removing work from the wheel

Removing your work from the wheelhead is as crucial an operation as any other part of throwing, since even the best thrown pots can be ruined by careless removal. Just as throwing techniques vary according to the shape of the form being made, personal preference and confidence apart, there are specific methods of removing work from the wheel that are suited to certain forms. Unless, of course, you use a removable wheel bat system, when all you need to do is slice the form free from the wheel bat and leave it until it is dry.

Flooding the wheelhead

1 This is the best way to remove your work if you are not working on a removable bat. Hold a cutting wire taut. It must not be too long because it might cut the base unevenly and make trimming difficult. Press the wire down on the far side of the wheelhead. Slide it towards you, under the pot.

2 Flood the wheelhead making sure that the water does not spill over into the pot. Slice under the pot with the wire again to force the water under the base.

3 Take a wet tile and hold it level with the surface of the wheelhead. The pot will slide on to the tile when pushed from its base. Repeat if it does not move easily.

Direct Lift
Remove any slurry from the outer base of the pot with a rib. Ensure that your hands are dry. Slice under the pot with a cutting wire. Take hold of the form as near the bottom as possible and with a gentle rocking motion, ease it off the wheelhead surface. Once you have mastered this method, you will be able to remove work quickly, and leave a clay pad in the middle of the wheelhead to which the next piece you throw will adhere.

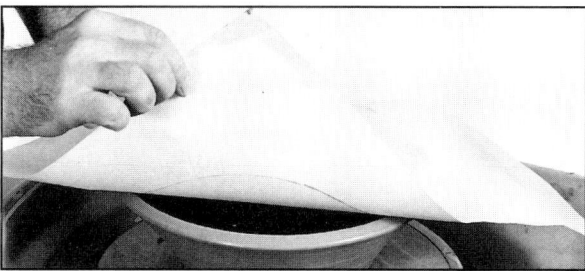

Removing the forms
Cut under the base with a wire and place a piece of paper across the top of the form. Seal its edges to the rim. The paper will trap the air within the form and help it to keep its shape when it is gently lifted off the wheel bat.

Removing delicate forms
Some forms are difficult, if not impossible, to move when they are soft. Drying them off slightly with a hairdryer will help. Ensure that your hands are dry, rotate the wheel and direct the hairdryer on to the clay to stiffen it.

Repetition throwing and sets

Whether they aspire to work in professional production, or whether they simply want to make a single set of coffee mugs, most potters will find it useful to be able to throw a number of items of a similar size and related shape. There are several simple rules to follow during repetition throwing. The first most obvious one is to weigh out the clay in equal amounts. The next is to keep the shape you throw simple so that it is possible to repeat it without too much effort. Although speed is not always essential, taking a long time to try and capture a certain shape can result in tired-looking end results. A simple shape does not have to be a dull or unimaginative shape; it can often be exciting and fresh where complex shapes seem contrived and over-fussy.

While it is easy to produce a template for the profile of any shape to act as a guide when throwing a set, forms thrown in this way can often look suspiciously unoriginal. Obviously it is a matter of personal preference whether or not to rely simply on your hands and a few simple tools, and potters who practise either of these methods may find the alternative completely abhorrent. The crucial thing to remember is that the use of templates will always alter the finish of the form; it will not have a "thrown" surface and may look machine, rather than hand, made.

It is difficult to achieve any real fluidity of shape through repetition throwing if you are only producing half a dozen or so objects. Try to go and watch a professional potter who produces hundreds of similarly shaped items every week, and you will see repetition throwing at its best — each form retains its individuality and yet fits into a batch as one of many.

Sets

Throwing a number of similar forms does not necessarily imply that you have made a set. In a coffee set, for example, the mugs or the sugar bowl will not be the same as the pot or the jug, but the pieces should have enough common characteristics to show that they all go together. Achieving this corporate unity entails careful design consideration at the earliest stages. Although the size of the components vary, their shapes relate to each other in definite ways. It is often true that the components in a set, when examined closely, are unique in design; it is only a general characteristic that distinguishes all the pieces as "belonging". Decoration and the chosen glaze of course assist in the distinction of the pieces you make, and although not within the scope of this book, these should be borne in mind when you make plans to throw a set.

1 Once you have thrown your "pattern" shape, place it nearby at eye level so that you can see its profile from the wheel. There are several types of measuring gauges that can be used to record the dimensions of height and width.

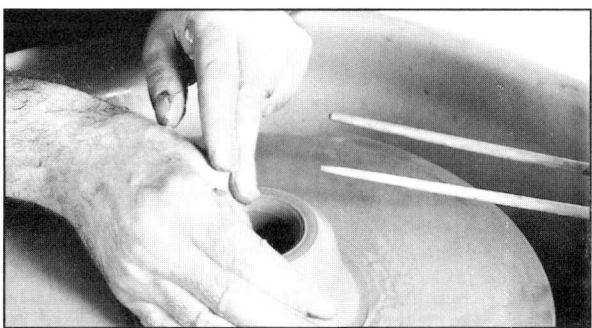

2 Calipers or a ruler, however, are often all that is required. The simplest way to keep a check on dimensions is to set a stick stuck into a piece of clay onto the side of the wheel tray at the height of the first shape.

34

The Potter's Projects

Salt pigs

Apart from their obvious functional uses in the kitchen, the two basic pig shapes shown in this project — a tall, straight-sided cylinder and a large enclosed form — involve useful techniques to learn from. The forms also lend themselves to many other ideas. The enclosed form, for example, might effectively be adapted to accommodate a trailing plant. With a looped handle it could be suspended.

Style A

1 Centre 3.5kg (7lbs) of clay and throw a fairly sturdy cylinder, *(see pp. 20–21)* Once the walls are sufficiently high, trim off the ragged edge of the rim with a needle. Gently press the rim to flatten and thicken it and smooth your throwing rib up the side of the form, supporting from the inside as you go. This will make the surface of the form compact and even, *(see diag)*. Impress a cuff into the rim with the tip of your right forefinger. Smooth the rim with a sponge and mop out any water with a sponge attached to a stick while the wheel is still rotating. △

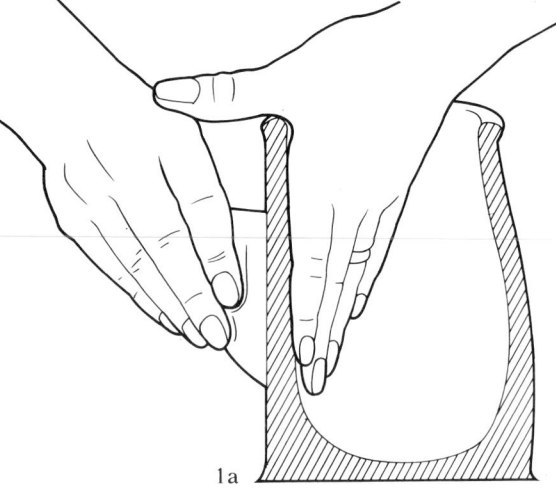

1a

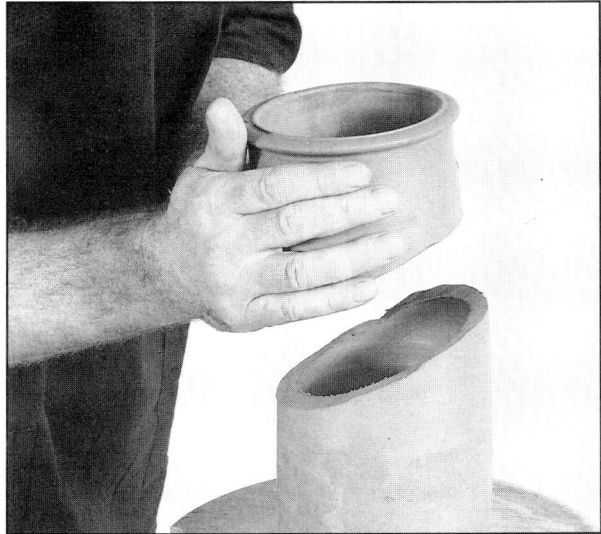

2 Tidy any waste clay away from the base of the cylinder with a trimming tool and leave the form to dry to leather hard. Hold a cutting wire taut and pull it firmly towards you through the cylinder at an angle of 30°, one third of the way down the form.

3 Score the cut surfaces of both pieces with a knife to ensure a good bond when they are joined with a slurry. Apply the slurry to the edges of both pieces. △

4 Join the pieces together, turning the upper portion through 180° so that when in place it protrudes away at an angle to the main body of the form. Smooth the outer join and place a narrow coil of clay inside it to cover and seal the inner join. Pull a handle and leave it until it has stiffened but pliable. ◁

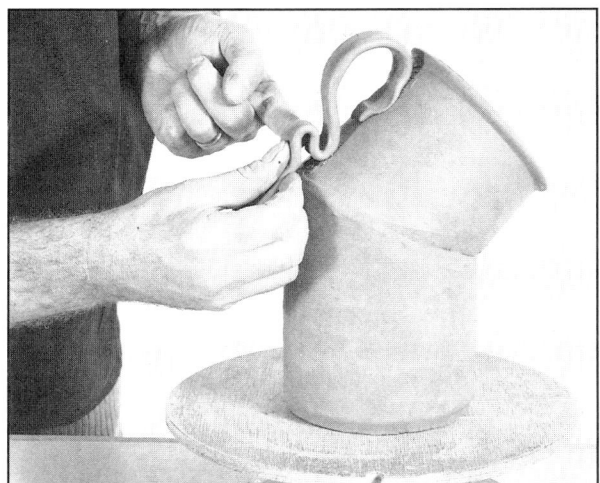

5 Mark the position of the handle on the back of the upper section of the pig. Score this area and apply slurry. Attach the handle, forming a generous curve. △

6 Make the decorative curves at the base and head of the handle with the excess clay pulled for the handle. Bend the strips into loops and smooth the ends on to the body of the pig. Using a wooden scorer, accentuate the position of the handle by incising lines down the sides of the pig. ▷

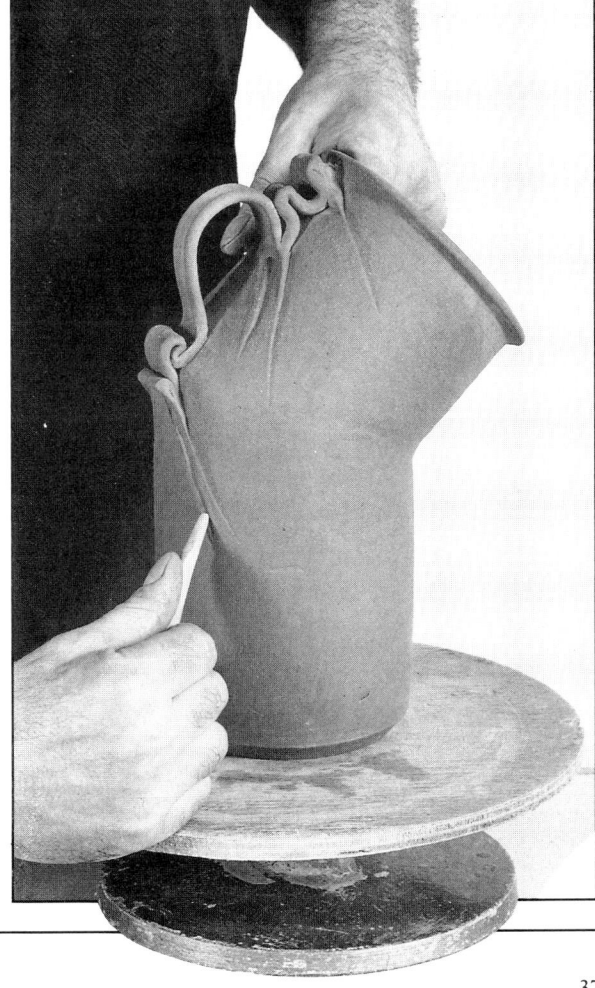

Style B

1 Again, use 4.5kg (7lbs) of clay. Throw a cylinder of the same size as before, but during the first lift, begin to exert pressure inwards as you approach the top to form a rounded head. ▽

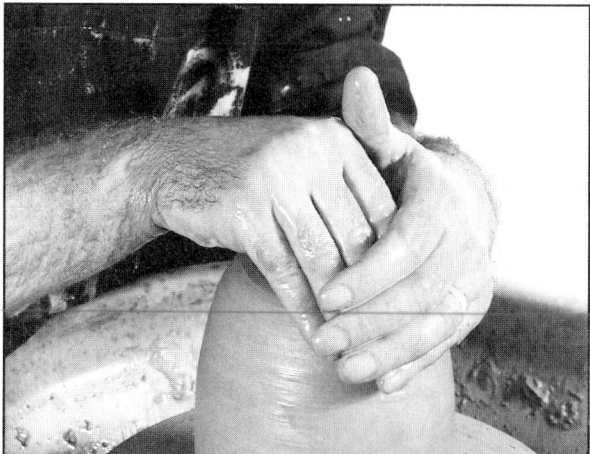

2 Collar the top and △ continue to lift the walls remembering that you will eventually close the top over. Mop up the water inside the form with a sponge attached to a stick.

3 Steady the form with both hands and your arms braced on the wheel tray. Once the walls have thinned out, start to collar at the top until the form actually closes. ▽

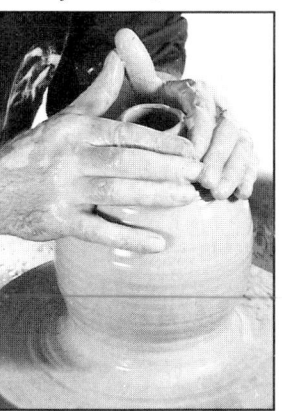

4 Remove the excess clay from the top with a pin and seal the wall join over with your fingertips. Once it is sealed, the shape can be modified from the exterior. Trim the excess clay away from the base and smooth up the sides of the form with the throwing rib.

Making the collar

1 To make the entrance collar, centre 0.6kg (1¼lbs) of clay and flatten it into a low dome. Press the tip of your thumb down through the dome to the wheelhead. Insert both thumbs into this cavity and open the clay. Raise the rim and compress it. For a decorative effect, trim the rim with a needle and lightly indent its flattened surface. Smooth the rim with a sponge, and the walls with the rib. △

2 Remove the collar from the wheelhead and squash it gently into an oval shape. Leave it until it is leather hard.

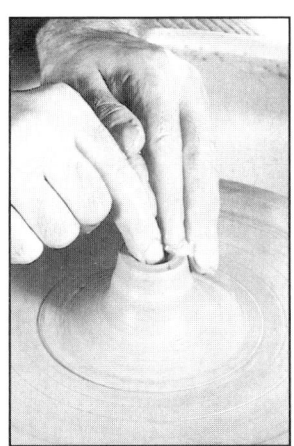

Making the knob

1 To make the knob, centre a small piece of clay and raise it into a small cone. Plumb straight down in the centre of it with your right forefinger until you reach the surface of the wheelhead. △

2 Raise the wall by gripping the clay between the forefinger and thumb of your right hand. Support the outside wall with your left hand, and gradually collar the shape over. Close the top of the hollow inner column to form a central bulge.

3 Create a comfortable grip on the knob by squeezing gently around the middle section of this small column.

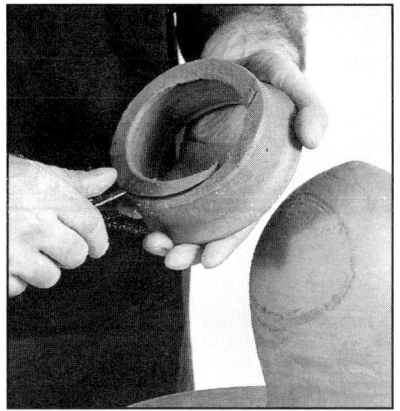

Final Construction

1 To attach the entrance collar, mark the surface of the form with the base of the oval. Shape the inner surface of the oval collar at an angle so that it fits snugly over the curve of the form. △

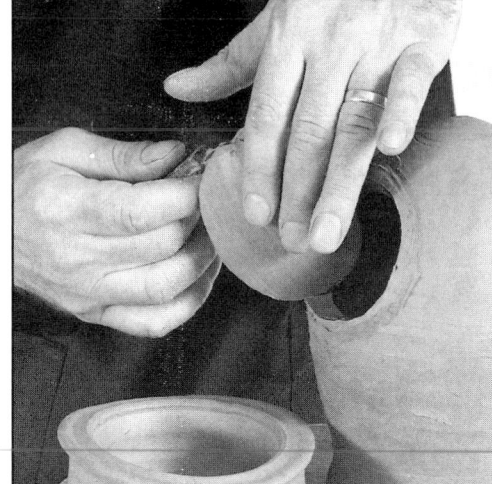

2 Cut out a slightly smaller oval shape from the wall of the form, using the mark on the clay surface as a guideline. Score both the surfaces to be joined and apply slurry. Press the oval collar in place on the form. Tidy up the inside of the entrance with a knife or a finger and smooth the join over with your fingertips. Smooth the outer join in the same way. Wipe over the joins, inner and outer, to ensure that they are well sealed.

3 To attach the knob, make a hole in the apex of the form with a piercing tool to release the air pressure inside the form, and place the knob over it. △

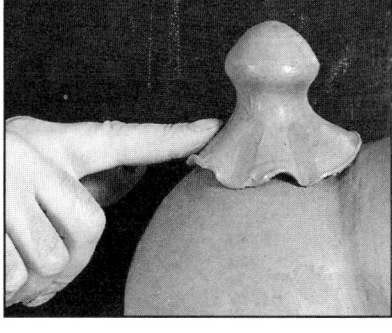

4 Ease the flared outer lip of the knob down on to the pig and shape it with your fingers to create a fluted effect. ◁

5 Impress the sides of the pig with a wooden roller to add interest to its surface. To complete the decoration of the pig, add small pellets of clay at the base of each indent around the pig and smooth them up with your forefinger to form a petal decoration.

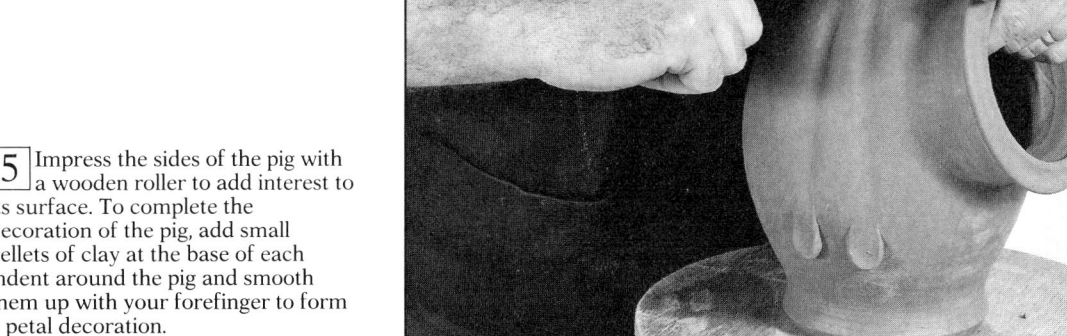

Salt pigs

Very attractive results can be obtained by pouring a lighter glaze over a darker one. When one glaze is poured over another, as in this instance, you must ensure that the final glaze is not too thick or it will run during firing.

Spice jars

The interesting aspect of these jars is that lid and base are thrown as one form. There is no reason why you should not use the same technique to make jars of different sizes. You could also alter the proportions of the lid and knob in relation to the size of the jar. The technique is ideal for making shallow pill-boxes, without incorporating a knob into the design.

1 Centre 1kg (2lbs) of well-prepared clay and throw a straight sided cylinder. With consecutive lifts, begin to close the shape in. You will need to raise the form to a higher level eventually, but try not to open out the neck as you do so.

2 Use two fingers of your left hand within the shape instead of your whole hand, resting your remaining fingers on your supporting right hand. Mop out any water using a sponge on a stick while the wheel is still rotating.

3 Because the shape has been collared, there will be plenty of clay to work with in the upper section of the pot. This extra thickness will be important when you start to form the knob. Close the form over when the walls are the right height.

4 The pressure exerted against the clay walls by the air trapped within the form allows you to mould the pot without worrying that the form will collapse. Begin to shape the knob by collaring gently at the apex of the pot.

5 Make sure that the walls of the pot are straight in the section where the lid will eventually meet the base. Use a rib to straighten off any unevenness in this area and smooth down the clay. Remove any waste clay from the base.

6 Using a small rectangular piece of wood, start to dig into the wall at the point where you want the lid segment to begin, forming a smooth indentation. Use a rib to ensure that the walls of the pot and lid are level. Even off any ragged edges and leave the pot to dry to leather hard.

7 Recentre the pot, securing it with small pieces of clay. When the piece dries it will shrink and the air pressure inside it will build up and may distort the form. To prevent this, pierce the side of the form with a needle. Use the needle to cut through the wall at the point where the pot juts out under the indentation to release the lid.

8 Trim off the rim of the pot with a needle. Use the pot cavity as a chuck for trimming the lid.

9 Invert the lid into the pot and secure it with small pieces of clay. Trim off any ragged edges on the lid flange with a trimming tool to ensure that the lid fits into the pot.

10 Put the lid the right way up on the pot and trim the walls flush. At this stage you can also shape the knob and make a decorative feature of the lid's rim by trimming into the swell.

11 Turn the base of the jar and pare off its edges at an angle of 45°. Hollow out a central indentation and smooth the whole jar off with a sponge.

Spice jars

A warm-coloured glaze would seem to be the most appropriate for a set of jars which contain various spicy, tangy substances. The shiny finish provides an extra touch of luxury.

Cheese dish

The technique used for making the cover of the dish can be adapted to make a plant container, hung upside down in a macrame hanging, or even a large lid for a meat dish, with the addition of a separately formed handle.

1 To make the cover of the dish, centre 2.5kg (5lbs) of clay. Flatten the clay out until you reach the circumference you want to work to. Push your thumbs down through the clay to the wheelhead and open the form.

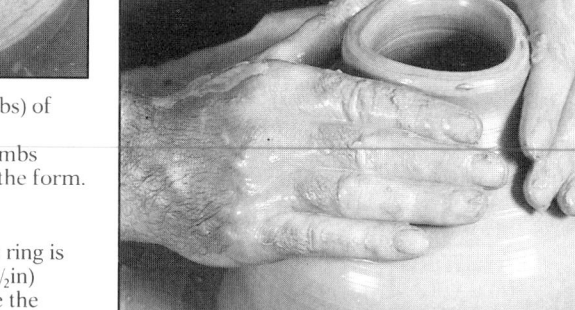

2 When the clay ring is about 1.3cm ($\frac{1}{2}$in) thick, begin to raise the walls. You should aim to produce a rounded bell-shape. As you near the top, reach into the form through its narrowed opening to finalize the swelling. ▷

3 Collar the top of the form, producing a good thickness of clay from which to develop the handle. Ensure that the handle you throw affords a good grip. Trim off any unevenness on the rim with a needle. If you wish you can close the open end of the handle with a small pellet of clay. ◁

4 Smooth off the outer walls of the cover using a rib. Trim away any waste clay from the base and use your trimming tool at the same time to accentuate the lower lip of the cover. ▷

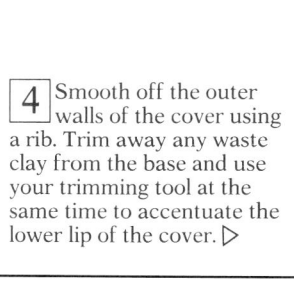

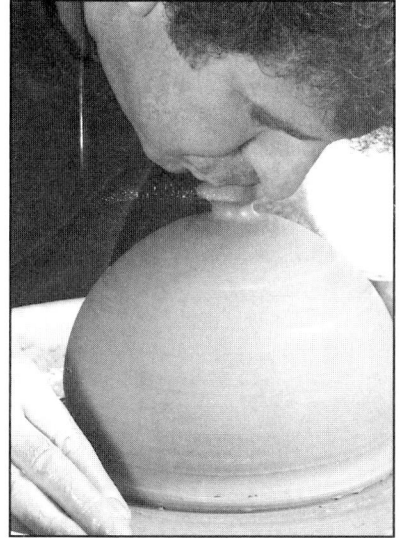

5 You can inflate the dome shape of the cover by blowing gently into it through the handle spout to produce an even shape. Measure the diameter of the cover so that you know how wide to make the dish. The lid will sit inside the rim of the dish. △

6 Trim the cover once it is leather hard. Invert it into a plastic basin that has been secured to the wheelhead with small pellets of clay. Roll a thick clay coil and wrap it around the rim of the cover to cushion it during trimming.

7 To finish off the cover, paint bands of different widths around it with coloured slip. Firstly, paint a wide band of thick slip around the middle section of the cover. Then with a fine brush paint slimmer decorative lines around the rim, the lip of the handle and the top of the cover bell.

8 Using a piece of stiff card or hardboard with teeth cut into one end, rotate the wheel and scratch a surface pattern into the slip before it dries. The scratching will expose the lighter colour of the clay beneath the slip and produce an attractive design. Brush off any excess slip scratchings when the cover has dried.

Making the dish

1 To make the dish, centre 2kg (4 lbs) of clay. Begin to spread the clay, checking the diameter measurement as you do so. Form a low ridge around the circumference of the flattened shape.

2 Steady the outer wall of the ridge as you establish the dish shape. Once you have reached the required diameter, refine the shape of the dish.

3 Use a throwing rib to develop a good, firm shape. The rib smooths the surface of the dish and gives clear-cut edge to its inner curve.

4 Bend the rim of the dish gently outwards, supporting the base of the form with your left hand as you ease over the clay with your right.

5 Having smoothed the dish and trimmed away any waste clay at its base, leave it to dry to leather hard. Using coloured slip as described on p. 47, you can decorate its rim with a design that complements the cover.

Cheese dish

A darkly coloured slip can usually be relied upon to bleed through a light coloured glaze such as the one used to complete this piece. The slipped combed pattern, although slightly obscured by the glaze, remains visible.

Egg cup stand

When they are examined, many seemingly complex forms prove to be no more than a combination of simple shapes. This egg cup stand combines simple throwing skills to produce an unusual functional item.

1 Centre 3.5kg (7lbs) of clay. Open the clay out with the tips of both thumbs, keeping the emerging base flat, until it almost reaches the width of the wheelhead. Steady the clay wall with your palms. ◁

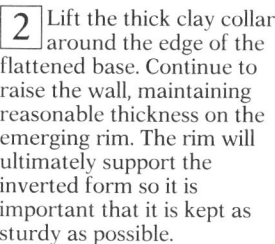

2 Lift the thick clay collar around the edge of the flattened base. Continue to raise the wall, maintaining reasonable thickness on the emerging rim. The rim will ultimately support the inverted form so it is important that it is kept as sturdy as possible.

3 Trim off any unevenness before compressing the rim. Remove any water from within the form with a sponge and trim away any excess clay from around the base. △

4 Once the form has dried to leather hard, invert and centre it on the wheelhead, and secure it with small clay pellets. Begin to turn the base, remembering that the surface you are smoothing down is actually the top surface of the form. Work outwards flattening the clay and leave a small ridge around the edge of the upper area. Smooth the form with a damp sponge.

6 The holes should be made slightly larger than is necessary because they will shrink during firing. Cut out the holes, starting them with a piercing tool and finishing with a needle. Angle the sides of the cuts slightly and smooth them with a sponge. Tidy the inside of the stand.

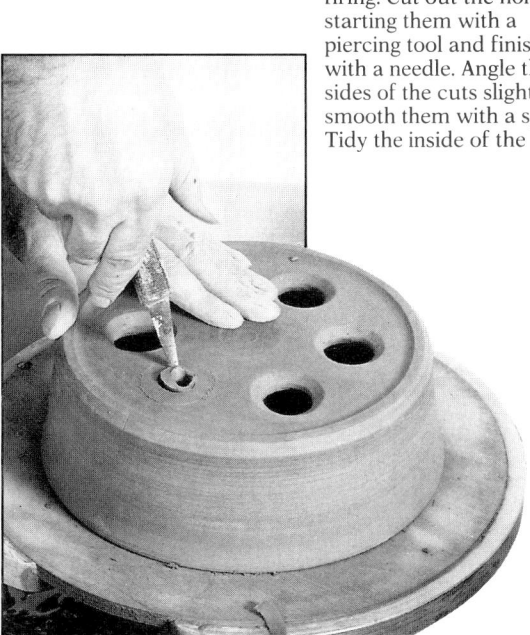

5 The six holes in which the egg cups will sit should be cut out at regular points around the circumference of the stand. To divide the circular area into six, take a piece of string and wrap it around the rim of the form, then divide the string, by folding, into sixths. Place a sixth of the string length as a measuring guide around the circumference and mark the clay either side of it. Score lines across the surface of the stand, joining each mark around the circumference with its opposite number. These lines divide the circle up into six equal parts. Each line will exactly bissect the holes made for the egg cups. Draw around a suitable circular object to mark out the six holes. △

Alternative Designs

There are various styles of handle that would be suitable for this stand – basket handles at each side of the form or a single handle bridging its width for example. Extrude several handle lengths from soft clay. For the "bridge-style" handle, flatten the clay length and loop it across the stand, dipping it to join the stand at the exact centre. Score the appropriate areas of both stand and handle, apply slurry and press the handle firmly into place.

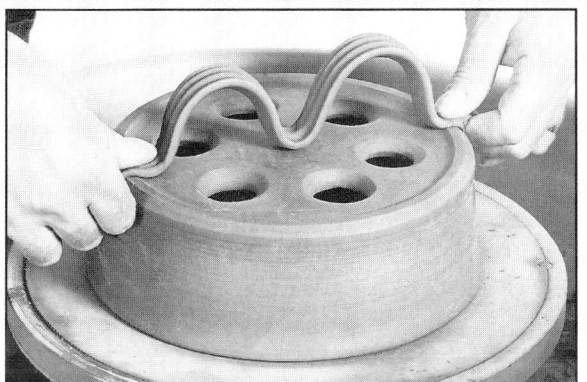

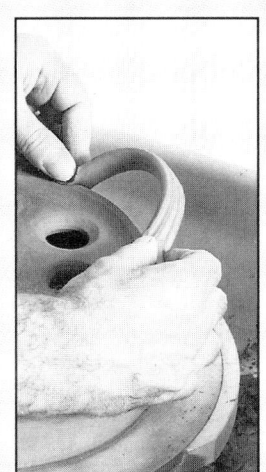

For the basket handles, shape two suitable handle lengths. With slurry, attach them to opposite sides of the stand. Angle the handles to point slightly upwards.

Making the handle

1 Centre 350g (12oz) of clay and throw a small cylinder, plumbing down to the wheelhead with your thumb. Once the basic cylinder shape has emerged, you can shape it as you wish, remembering to ensure that the shape you produce is comfortable to grip. Trim around the base of the knob, reflecting the angular quality of the base. Smooth over the whole form with a damp sponge.

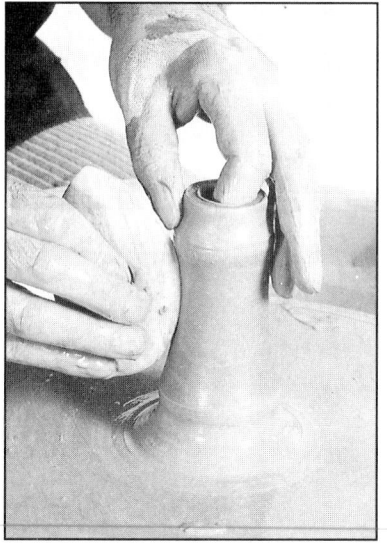

2 When the knob has dried to leather hard, score the central area of the stand where it is to be attached, apply slurry and press the knob firmly into place. Smooth the join over using a wooden tool to firmly seal the edge of the knob to the surface of the stand. ▷

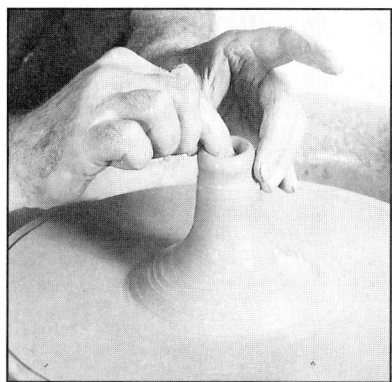

Making the egg cups

1 The matching egg cups are made by stack-throwing. Centre a piece of clay of a size that you can comfortably manage on the wheel and begin to throw a series of small bowls. Keep their rims to a delicate thickness and ensure that they are large enough to hold an egg.

2 Shape the foot of each bowl before slicing it from the stack of clay so that the cups have good stems.

Trim around the swell of the cups once they have dried to leather hard so that they fit snugly in the stand.

Egg cup stand

A rust-coloured glaze has been used on this piece of work.
Wax resist emulsion was then brushed over the surface to
produce a simple pattern and a lighter shiny glaze was
applied.

Hors d'oeuvres tray and dishes

A simple shallow open form is arguably one of the easiest forms to throw on the wheel. Once centred and opened, one simple lift of the wall is required and since it has a low profile, no problems with stability should arise. With a little ingenuity, however, even this simple form can be used to good effect.

1 Centre 4.5g (9lbs) of clay. Once it is centred, spread the clay out on the wheelhead to form a flattened shape using the palm of your right hand and supporting the widening outer rim of the clay with your left. Spread the circular disc wide enough to form a generous tray base, but keep it thick so that a wall can be lifted around its circumference.

2 Open the form out with both thumbs, supporting the clay as it spreads with your palms. Push outwards evenly within the cavity. Press down on the growing rim with your left thumb to prevent it splitting.

3 Continue working the rim out until it protrudes about 2.5cm (1in) beyond the base. Mop out the water in the cavity with a sponge. Lift the rim wall very slightly and straighten it.

4 When the rim is sufficiently formed, compress the outer lip of the tray. To make a feature of the rim, part split it with your fingernail. Smooth the indentation formed with a damp sponge to make a rounded edge. Remove any excess clay from around the base, remembering as you do that the base has to be wide enough to support the tray.

5 Mark out quarters around the edge of the tray with your fingertip as the first step towards reshaping the tray. Once your four "corner" marks are in place, gently tease the rim outwards with your right forefinger at each of these four points — almost as if you were making a spout. Support the clay wall with the thumb and finger of your other hand as you go. This decorative moulding defines the areas within the tray in which the dishes will ultimately fit. As an alternative, you can angle these curves inwards. Once the clay has stiffened slightly, the shape can be reinforced to ensure a well-defined shape.

7 Take two sections of pulled handle and attach them in generous loops to opposite sides of the tray's rim between two curved corners.

6 When the tray has dried to leather hard, invert it on to the wheelhead and secure it with clay pellets. turn the base as usual to ensure that the under surface is well flattened. A wide shallow form requires two supporting footrings to prevent it sagging. Define the position of the two rings with the point of a turning tool and work them up, starting at the outeredge. Smooth off the surface with a sponge.

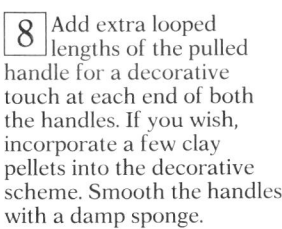

8 Add extra looped lengths of the pulled handle for a decorative touch at each end of both the handles. If you wish, incorporate a few clay pellets into the decorative scheme. Smooth the handles with a damp sponge.

Making the dishes

1 The four hors d'oeuvres dishes are each made from 0.5kg (1lb) of clay. Once the clay is centred, flatten it down into a domed shape.

2 Make a simple shallow form and raise the walls very slightly. Gently flatten the rim and impress a slight ridge in it with your fingernail, so that the design of the dishes echoes that of the tray. Smooth off the rim.

3 Trim away any excess clay around the base of the dish. When you have sliced the dish off the wheelhead with a wire, gently compress its circular shape into a triangle. This is important if the dishes are to fit snugly into the tray.

4 Once the dishes are leather hard, you can pare off any unwanted clay from the base edges with a sharp knife.

Hors d'oeuvres tray and dishes

A simple opaque white glaze was used on the tray and the matching dishes. Iron oxide has been brushed over the rim surfaces of the tray and all the dishes to accentuate their design details.

Teapots, cups and saucers

When making a tea-set, a single overall design has to be kept in mind when you begin to throw any one of its components. The shape of the teapot should relate to that of the cups and saucers. Two types of teapot construction are described in this project, both with a different lid fitting. The character of the teapot can be altered completely by the style of its lid. These lid fittings can be used for a variety of different forms.

Teapot A

1 Centre 2kg (4lbs) of clay for the body of the pot. Begin to encourage a rounded shape as you raise the wall of the clay, modifying the swell as the wall grows. ◁

2 Begin to curve and close the upper section over by easing the clay gently from within the form. Sit back from the wheel to check that the shape is balanced and developing as required. Finalize the swell of the pot by lifting the clay out and up from the bottom of the form.

3 Collar the neck of the pot, impressing a ledge on which the cup lid will rest. Remove any water from within the form. Throw the thickened rim of the ledge so that a narrow upper wall emerges. Trim off the rim with a needle or a pin. △

4 With a lubricated throwing rib, define the walls of the upper section and the ledge so that the lid will fit snugly over the top. Trim any excess clay from around the base.

5 Measure the exterior diameter of the rim using calipers so that you know the right measurement for the inner diameter of the cup lid when you come to throw it.

6 When the teapot has dried to leather hard, turn any excess clay from its base using a trimming tool. This stage also refines the profile of the pot.

Decorating the teapot

This teapot will look even more attractive with some simple decoration – fluting for example. This decoration is best applied when the walls of the teapot are soft leather hard, before you attach the spout. Fluting undertaken at this stage minimizes the risk of deforming the pot and produces cleaner lines.

Define the area of the pot to be fluted by marking lines circling the sides, (right). Use a fluting tool – a length of wood pared flat at one end will do just as well – and press it into the side of the teapot at the level of the lower line. Gently draw the tool up the side of the pot, either straight or at a slant, (far right), until

you reach the upper line. The clay will peel off in strips. Smooth over the pot with a damp sponge. This decoration will add interest to any style of teapot you choose to make.

Making the lid

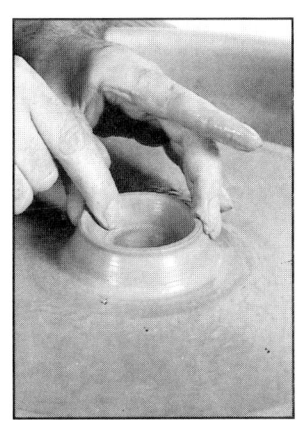 

1 Centre 170g (6oz) of clay and throw a very small bowl. Check the inner diameter measurement and stop opening the clay when you reach the right width.

2 Raise a low wall around the shape and thicken its rim as a precaution against chipping. Smooth off the edges with a damp sponge.

3 Trim away any excess clay around the base to refine the curved shape. At this stage you can define the lid's eventual silhouette by trimming tight into the base of the bowl form.

4 When the lid is leather hard, secure it with clay pellets to the trimmed throat of the teapot and refine its curved shape. The lid should be trimmed until it is a good shape to handle easily.

Making the spout

1 The spout can be made when the pot and lid have dried a little because it will dry at a much faster rate. Centre 170g (6oz) of clay and form it into a cone. Plumb straight down to the wheelhead and begin to throw a thin conical cylinder.

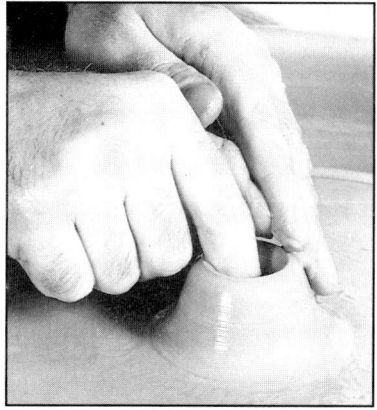

2 With each lift thin out and collar the top section of the cylinder, keeping the whole form as slim as you possibly can, but retaining width at the base.

3 With one finger, continue to lift and collar the rim. If the opening is too narrow to insert a finger, use a dowel or the handle of a brush.

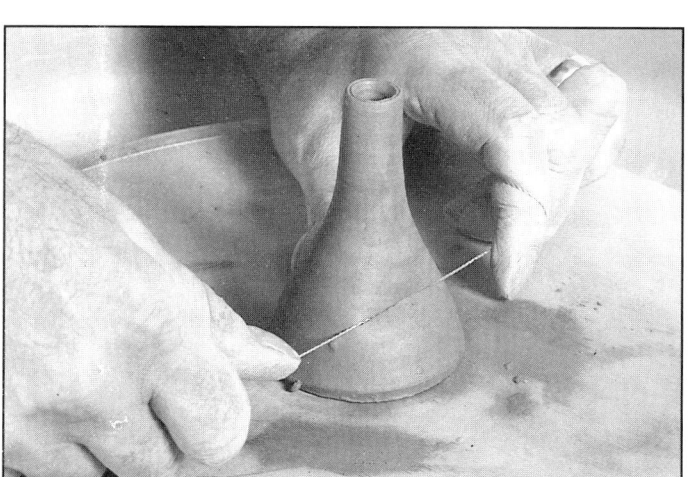

4 Flare the rim of the spout slightly. Trim away any waste clay from the base and leave it to dry to soft leather hard. To attach the spout, slice away a portion of its base at an angle. Measure the spout up with the body of the teapot to check its proportions and where to attach it.

5 The end of the spout should not be lower than the level of the lid, or tea will pour out as the pot is filled. Trim the sliced surface of the spout so that it fits smoothly on to the teapot. Once you are happy with the position of the spout, mark the teapot around the edge of it's base.

6 Using a piercing tool held at 45°, make several straining holes within the marked spout area. Score the cut surface of the spout and the marked area on the teapot. Apply slurry and attach the spout. Blow down the spout to unblock it. △

7 Smooth off the join between the two pieces using any suitable tool and a sponge. If necessary, add a coil of clay around the join and smooth it into place. Gently mould the bottom edge of the spout.

Alternative Spouts

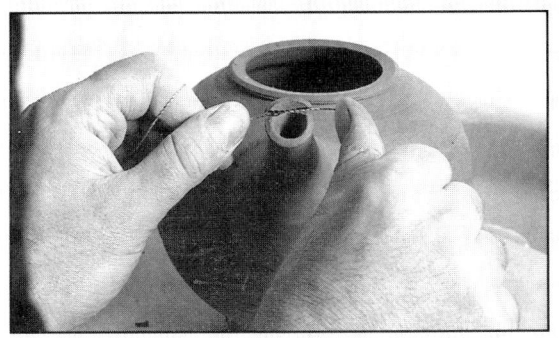

The end of the spout can be left as it is or it can be trimmed at a gentle angle using a taut wire. If you do slice off the end at an angle, slant your cut slightly to the left to counter the slight twist that firing will inevitably give to the spout.

Complete the shaping of the spout by easing the lower lip of the newly cut edge down. This angling of the lip assists pouring.

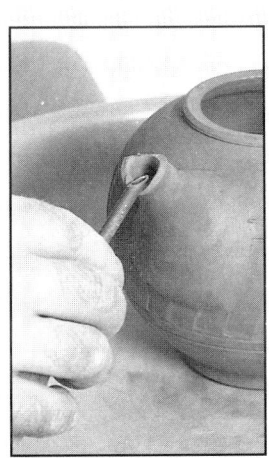

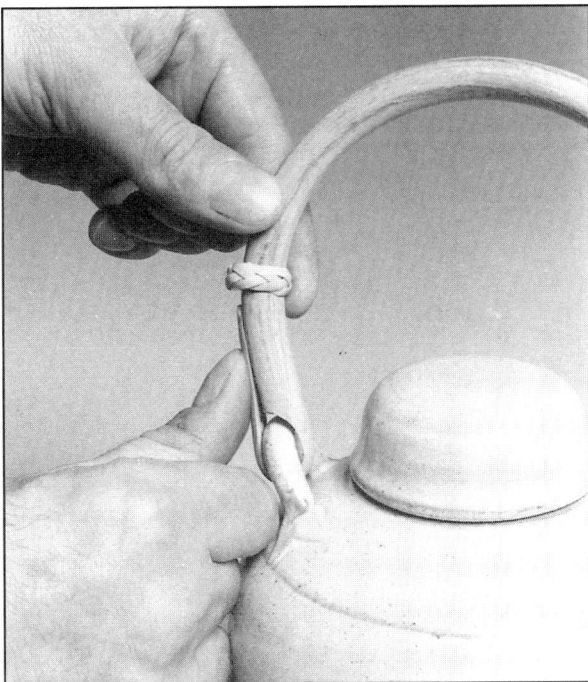

This style of teapot looks very attractive with a cane handle. Extrude or roll out two short coils of clay. Site the area directly above the teapot's spout in line with the centre of the lid and score it. Apply slurry to the ends of one of the coils and press it in place to form a loop over the spout. Repeat this process at the back of the teapot. Smooth small clay pellets over the joins to reinforce them.

Teapot B

1 Centre 2kg (4lbs) of clay and throw a full-bodied pot as you did for teapot A. Remove any water from within the pot before you narrow its throat too much. Collar and compress the rim simultaneously to ensure that it is thick enough for the lid to rest on.

2 Compress the wall of the pot using a throwing rib to smooth down the clay and strengthen the form. Trim away any excess clay from around the base.

3 Measure the diameter of the pot's throat so that you know how large to make the lid. The lid slot that sits within the throat will correspond with this measurement; the ledge of the lid will need to be about 1cm (²/₅in) wider. △

Making the lid

1 Centre 170g (6oz) of clay and open it by pressing into it with your forefinger at a point about 1cm (²/₅in) from the centre. A small pillar of clay will begin to emerge; the knob of the lid. ◁

2 Widen the outer edge of the lid and raise the wall slightly. Keep a careful check on the growing diameter as you throw and stop opening the shape once you have extended the edge of the form to the required measurement. △

4 Finish shaping the knob with your forefingers, increasing the size of its top to ensure that the lid can be easily gripped. Smooth the lid off with a sponge and trim away any excess clay from the base. Leave it to stiffen before you finalise any trimming and shaping. ▷

3 Begin to flatten and extend the outer wall of the lid over your right forefinger, keeping that finger steadily against the side of the lid to stop it spreading. Once the ledge has reached a suitable width, trim around its edge with a needle and smooth and compress its edge simultaneously with a damp sponge. △

5 Trim the teapot and lid once they are soft leather hard. The footring should be made fairly wide. Centre the teapot the right way up and secure it. Trim the neck of the pot so that the lid sits in it comfortably. Invert the lid, resting it carefully on the thickened pot rim, and secure it with clay pellets. Trim up the underside of the lid to ensure a neat fit. Throw a spout and attach it in the usual way. ◁

Attaching the handle

1 Extrude a handle to a suitable length. Score the area where the handle is to be joined to the pot, remembering to keep the spout, knob and handle aligned. Form the curve of the handle by lining it up with the teapot, and balancing its shape to the pot's swell. Apply slurry to the scored areas and attach the handle. △

2 Ensure that the joins are well bonded, reinforcing them with small rolls of clay. Press these rolls into the body of the teapot, and smooth the joins over with a sponge. △

3 To prevent the handle drooping as it dries, invert the teapot on a flat surface with the handle's upper curve hanging over the edge. ▷

Teapot C

1 Centre 2kg (4lbs) of clay and again throw a round-bellied pot, this time with a thickened rim. Lift a low wall around the rim. Compress it slightly and then split it with your fingertip, using your left hand to support your right.

2 Using a suitable implement, carefully push the inner side of the split clay down into the neck of the pot to form an internal gallery. Smooth off and adjust the shape of the rim above the gallery. Turn the teapot once it has dried to leather hard.

2 With your thumb nail, split the rim and extend the outer edge to form the flange; trim its edge with a needle. Raise the inner wall and form a slight spout to keep the lid in place when it is sitting in the throat of the teapot. Trim the wall so that it is slightly smaller than the width of the teapot; this ensures that it is easy to lift in and out.

Making the lid

1 Centre 170g (6oz) of clay and open it out, retaining a thick outer edge. Measure the diameter to check that you have reached the correct width before you begin to make the flange.

3 When the lid is leather hard, trim it down and add a knob. Begin to trim away the clay moving from the centre of the lid to its edge. When you have trimmed it down to a dome shape, define a circular area over the apex. Score this circle and apply a little slurry over the clay. The knob will be thrown from a lump of clay attached at this point.

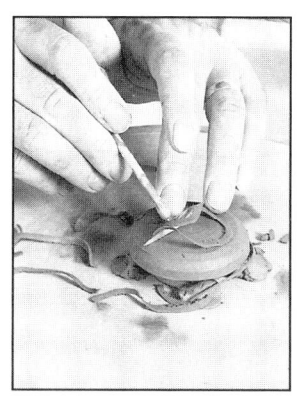

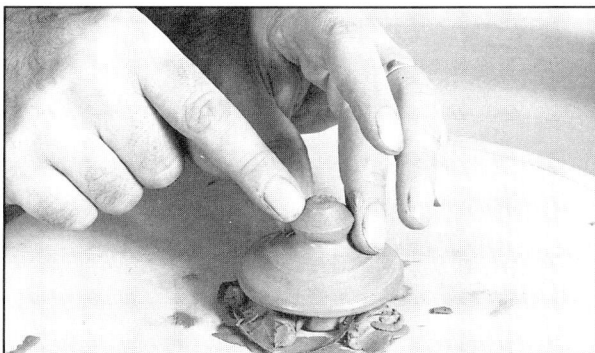

4 Score the base of a small cone of clay and attach it over the scored area of the lid. Smooth down the clay to make a firm join. Extend and shape the knob until it is the right size to grip easily. Pierce the lid above its internal lip. Attach a spout and a handle to the teapot as usual.

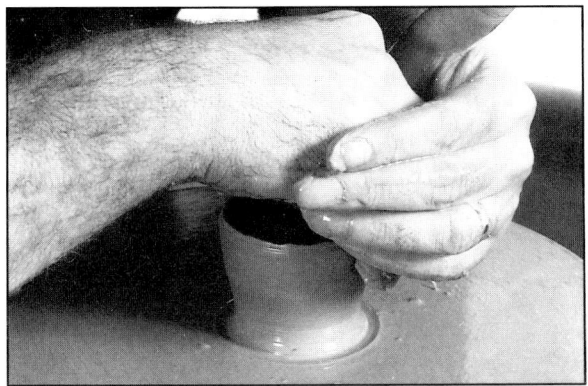

Making the teacups

1 For each cup, centre 0.2kg (½lb) of clay. Lift up a small dome with a narrow base. Begin to open out the dome, bearing in mind the shape of the teapot.

2 As the walls swell and grow, keep the foot of the cup reasonably narrow. The rim of the cup should be thick enough to withstand everyday wear and tear, but slim enough to be pleasant to drink from. Gently compress the rim with your fingertip. Trim away any excess clay from the base.

3 Measure both the diameter of the cup's foot and the diameter of its rim. The smaller measurement will act as a guide for the central indentation in the saucer, and the larger as a guide from which to work out the final diameter of the saucer. The saucers will be 6.8cm (2½ins) wider than the widest diameter of the cups.

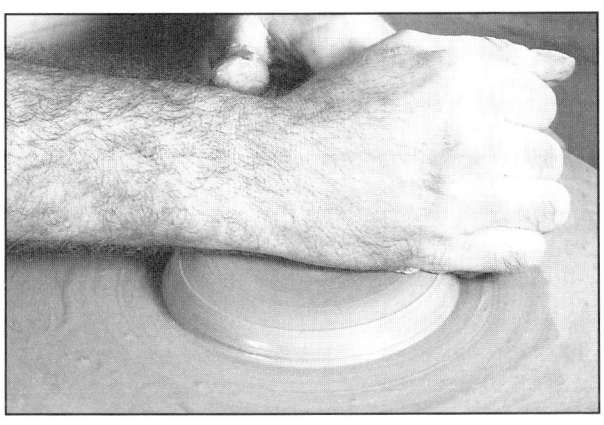

2 Begin to lift the edges of the disc into a gentle curve. Do not raise this rim too much; you must leave enough space for the handle of the cup. Smooth the shape with a sponge, thickening the edge as you do so. Using a suitable tool roughly mark out the central area for the cup to stand in.

Making the saucers

1 For each saucer, centre 395g (14oz) of clay. Press the clay down into a shallow flattened disc and begin to open it. Check the cup diameter measurement as you go.

Trimming the cup and saucer

1 When the cup has dried to leather hard, invert it on to the wheelhead and secure it with clay pellets. Trim the foot of the cup and take an accurate measurement of its diameter as a guide for making the saucer's indentation. ◁

2 When the saucer is leather hard you can finalise any trimming. Secure the saucer to the wheelhead and carefully pare away the clay from the centre to create an indentation of the required diameter. ▷

3 Then invert the saucer and turn its base to reduce its weight and refine its shape. Keep the footring narrow, but wide enough to keep the cup and saucer stable. Smooth over the surface of the saucer with a damp sponge.

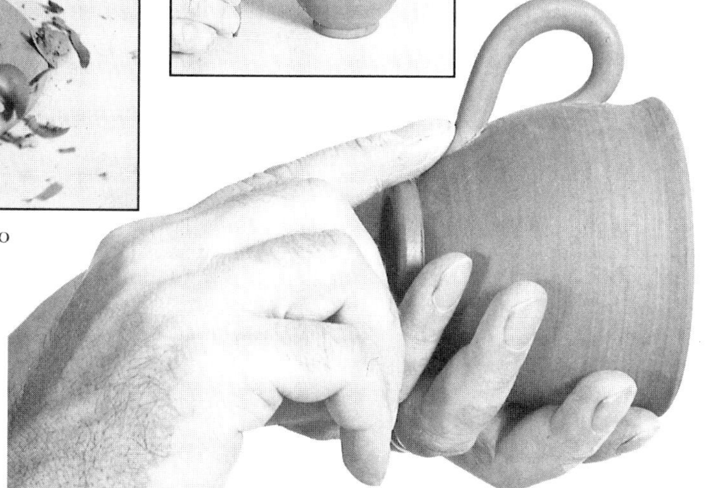

Attaching handles to the cups

Extrude suitable slender handles for the cups. Judge the right size of the handle loops by lining them up with the cups, (*top*). Apply slurry and press them into place in the usual way, smoothing the ends into the surface of the cups.

Teapots, cups and saucers

The glaze you choose for the teapots will alter their
appearance in the same way that variations in lid, handle
and spout design do. The decoration of the cups and saucers
should echo that of the pot.

Soup tureen and bowls

The bowl shape is one of beautiful simplicity and need not be difficult to throw. The best bowls, however, have a look of rounded fullness about them which seems to spring upwards from the foot. Regardless of size, the throwing technique is relatively simple, with the centrifugal force from the rotating wheelhead almost willing the shape to open out on its own. Consequently, only very gentle pressure is usually needed to swell the shape evenly.

1a

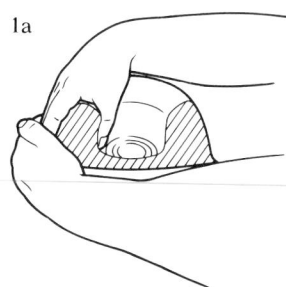

1 Centre 6kg (12lbs) of well-prepared clay to make the bowl. Open the clay and raise and swell the walls gently. Continue to exert pressure outwards as you lift, once the shape begins to emerge. ▷

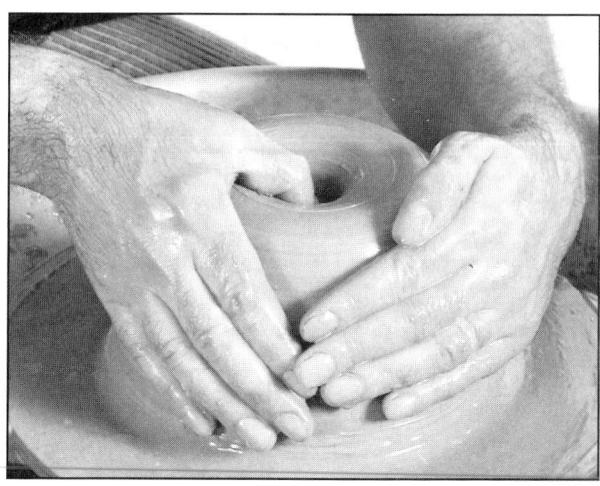

2 Bring up the thickness of the clay at the base of the bowl to add height to the form, but do not thin it down too much and reduce the basal support. ▷

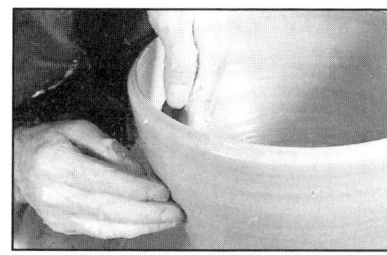

3 Once you have created the basic form, you can refine and modify it from within, carefully supporting the outer wall. Link up your hands when possible to maximize support. △

4 Trim the rim of the bowl with a needle to remove any unevenness. Compress the rim to give it a firm edge: this helps to stop the edge of the bowl chipping. Use a kidney to shape inside the bowl. Keep your hand steady as you do this by using your left hand to create a supporting bridge, bracing your arm into your sides. Trim away any waste clay.

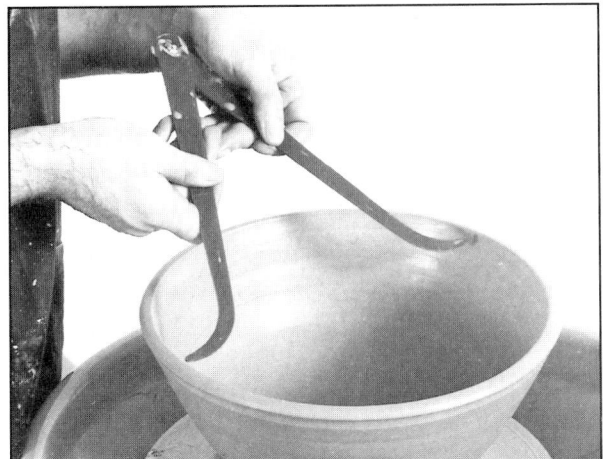

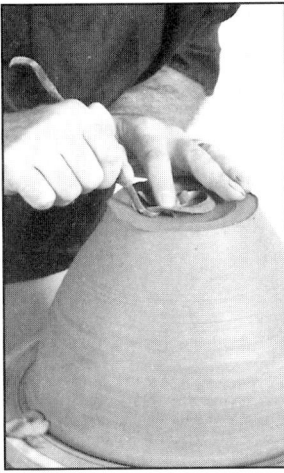

6 Invert the bowl, centre it on the wheelhead and secure it with clay. Trim the base flat, working from the centre outwards. Next, trim the edges and mark on the guidelines for the footring. Begin to shape the ring, working from the outer edge first.

5 Measure the diameter of the bowl with calipers so that you know how large the lid should be. Once it is leather hard, the bowl can be trimmed.

8 While the bowl is still leather hard you can attach its handles or lugs. Carefully mark around the handle curves on the sides of the tureen and score both these areas, and the underside of the lugs. Apply slurry and firmly mould the lugs on to the form.

7 Move to the centre and pare away the clay until the ring emerges. Smooth the base off with a sponge.

9 Draw the ends of the lugs together into a loop and sweep the flattened ends across each other and around the curve of the bowl. Carve the edges of the curves with a wooden scorer for additional emphasis.

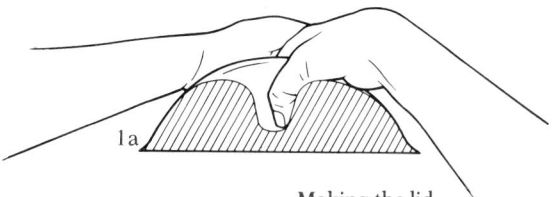

Making the lid

1 To make the lid of the tureen, centre 4.5kg (9lbs) of clay. Spread the centred clay into a wide-based dome of the required diameter. Open out the form, keeping a check on the width.

2 Continue to open out the form measuring its width with calipers from time to time. Begin to raise and shape the emerging wall as you enlarge the diameter.

3 Compress the rim to strengthen it and begin to split it with your fingernail. Trickle water down over your left hand to lubricate the clay and begin to press the outside edge of the rim gently downwards, supporting it underneath as the clay spreads to form a slim flange.

4 Define a 90° angle using a suitable tool. Mop out any water inside the form and smooth the flange with a sponge or strip of chamois leather.

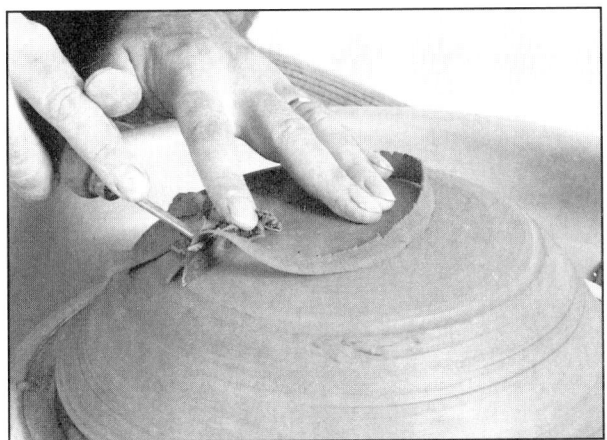

5 Once it has dried to leather hard, invert and centre the lid on the wheelhead. Trim away the clay to emphasize its domed shape, working down over the slope of the lid. Remove the most clay from the area corresponding to the point where the interior curve bends up to meet the rim: the area where the clay is at its thickest.

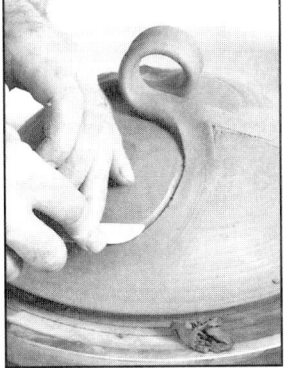

6 When the lid is still leather hard you can attach a handle at its apex. As well as being functional, handles can also be decorative and a style that is particularly attractive for a lid of this kind is a sturdy loop. Smooth both ends of the handle and swing them round to form a central loop. Score the area of the lid to which you are attaching the handle, and the underside of the handle itself. Apply slurry and join.

7 Once the handle is in position, you can incorporate it into the overall decorative design of the tureen. Split the two ends of the handle and spread the splits apart. Smooth the end handle clay down and around the lid, emphasizing the curve of the form as you go. Accentuate the curves using a wooden scorer.

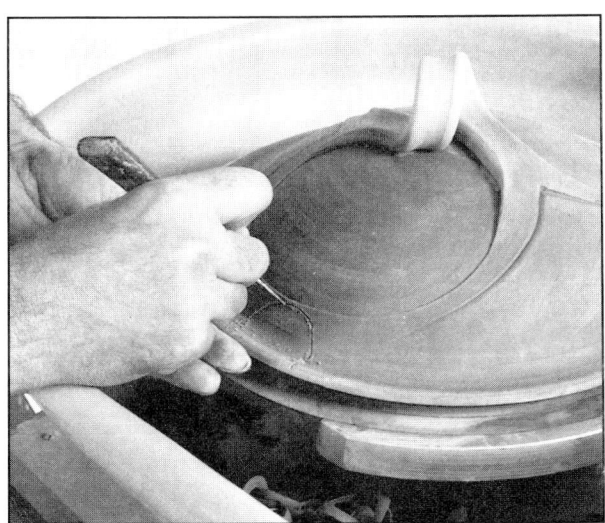

8 Cut out a deep semi-circle from the edge of the lid to allow the ladle handle to sit inside the tureen. Smooth off the edges of your cut.

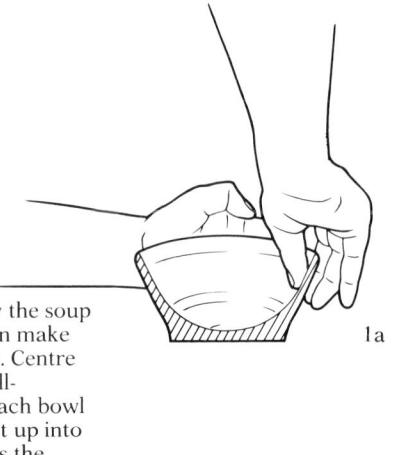

Making the bowls

1 To accompany the soup tureen, you can make several small bowls. Centre 0.7kg (1½lbs) of well-prepared clay for each bowl and begin to work it up into a shape that reflects the form of the soup tureen.

1a

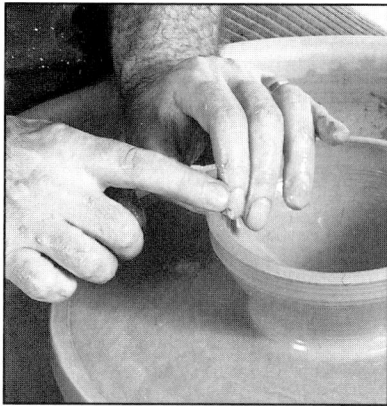

2 Begin by keeping the base of the bowl fairly narrow, and flare it out as you raise the wall. Keep plenty of thickness at the rim, to echo the edge of the tureen. When you have thrown the bowl to the right height, compress the rim.

3 Modify the shape of the bowl and refine its rim by paring the clay from the walls gently with a trimming tool. Trim away the waste clay at the base of the bowl to give the bowl a clean silhouette.

Making the ladle

1 For the ladle, throw a small round dish using 0.7kg (1½lbs) of clay. Keep the shape sturdy and the rim fairly thick.

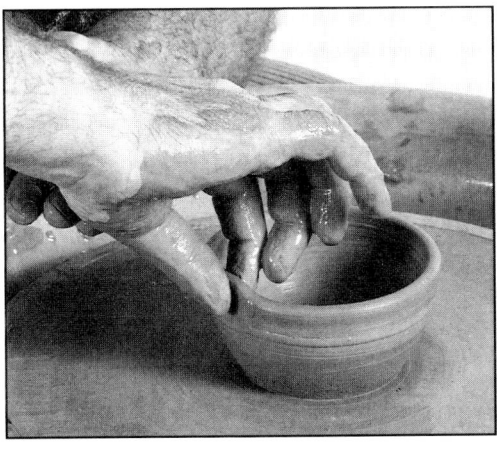

2 To make the pouring lip, slightly lift up a section of the lip with your thumb and forefinger. Pull the lifted clay outwards a little, keeping the wall of the ladle bowl steady with your other hand. Form a spout as you would on a jug.

3 Press the ladle bowl very gently to give it a slightly oval shape. Leave it to dry until it is leather hard.

4 The handle for the ladle should be left until it is still pliable but firm enough to maintain a long straight section. Once any trimming is complete, the handle can be fitted. Gently curl the end of the handle to form a good sized grip. Attach the handle with slurry having scored the surfaces to be joined.

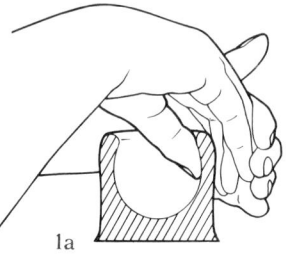

1a

Punch bowl and cups

1 The same methods can be used to make a punch bowl and cups set, but the cups will have to be made in a slightly different way. Use the same weight of clay as you did for the soup bowls, but when you begin to lift the form, remember to keep it narrower at its base — the cups need to be easy to hold.

2 Begin the cup from a narrow cone and allow it to rise straight for about 5cm (2in) before you begin to spread the cup out. As you pull the cup out, keep your arms braced on the wheel tray.

3 Compress and flare the rim slightly to give the cup a pleasant drinking edge. Trim in the base stem considerably to produce a slender stem shape.

4 You can make the punchbowl in the same way as you did the base of the soup tureen, without adding the lugs at the sides or throwing a lid. The ladle to serve the punch will be made in the same way.

Punch bowl set

A light, smooth textured glaze is probably the best choice for
this set, so that whatever the colour of your punch, it will
still look good. A dark brown glaze and cobalt oxide were
used for the pattern.

Casseroles

A ny item that requires the addition of separate components, such as lids, spouts or handles, should be designed with these components in mind. Casseroles are no exception, but there are also other equally important considerations to bear in mind when making them. Their shape must be stable and easy to serve from, and their handles or knobs must be easy to grip, even through an oven glove.

Style A

1 Centre 2.5kg (5lbs) of clay and open it out to the diameter you require for a casserole. Keep the base of the form fairly wide as you raise the walls. Swell the sides of the form keeping a good thickness of clay around the rim. △

2 Impress a cuff around the top of the casserole, to define a ridge below its rim and give it shape. Remove any water from within the casserole and trim any waste clay away from the base. Measure the diameter of the rim with calipers so that you know how wide to make the lid. △

3 When the casserole has dried to leather hard, invert it on the wheelhead and secure it with clay pellets. Turn the base, remembering that the footring should be wide enough to ensure that the casserole is stable. ◁

Making the lid

1 Centre 1.2kg (2½lbs) of clay and flatten it out to the diameter of the pot's rim. Open the clay, pushing your thumbs down to the wheelhead. Raise the walls of the form, tapering them at a point about 1.2cm (½in) above the wheelhead. Tease out a low ledge from the wall of this conical shape. ▷

2 To complete the lid, you have two options. You can collar the top of the conical cylinder, narrowing and refining its shape until it forms a knob that is easy and comfortable to grip. ◁

3 Alternatively you can seal the form over completely and then depress the dome of clay, forming a lid with a sunken centre.

4 Pierce the lid with a needle. This will release the air trapped with the form the clay and allow for further depressing of the central area.

5 Continue to shape the hollow until it is large enough to accommodate your hand when you grip the handle.

7 Carefully trim the centre of the lid to define the shallow central dome and ensure a good fit. Smooth over the trimmed form with a sponge.

6 When the lid has dried to leather hard, trim it so that it fits snugly into the neck of the casserole. Redefine the ledge by neatening it with a trimming tool held against the side of it at an angle of 90°.

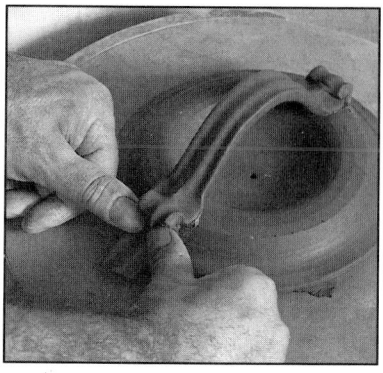

Making the handle

1 If you decided to make the lid with the sunken centre, you will need to attach a handle. Extrude or pull a handle to a suitable length and leave it to stiffen.

2 Score the lid at opposite points on the ridge surrounding the central dip. Apply slurry and press the scored ends of the handle into place, ensuring a generous arch across the lid. Reinforce the joins with loops of clay pressed under the handle ends. △

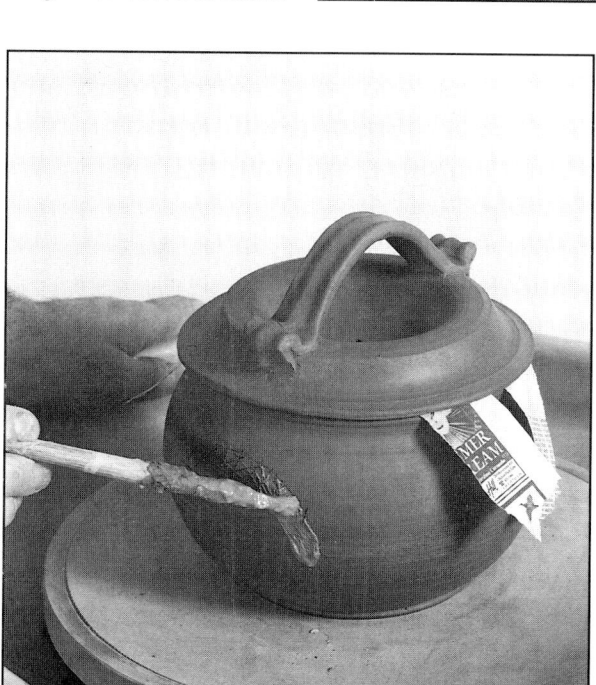

2 Press the lugs very firmly on to the wall of the casserole to ensure that they are bonded to the clay surface. If necessary reinforce the joins with small coils of clay. Smooth the joins with a damp sponge to seal them.

Attaching the lugs

1 Throw a low, baseless ring from 0.5kg (1lb) of clay. Slice this ring in half to form the two equal-sized lugs. Attach these lugs to the side of the casserole, first marking their position on the clay before scoring the surfaces to be joined and applying slurry.

Style B

1 Centre 1.5kg (3lbs) and throw a sturdy rounded pot in the same way as described for Casserole A, keeping a slightly thickened rim.

2 Raise the rim very slightly at the point on the circumference where you want to form the pouring lip. Form a pouring channel from the base upwards and ease the lip of this channel outwards. ◁

3 When the casserole has dried to leather hard, trim its base. Any vessel with a lip has to be cushioned with a clay coil when it is inverted. Measure the circumference of the casserole and draw a circle of the same size on the wheelhead. Make a thick clay coil to fit the circle. △

4 Flatten and trim the ring of clay and cut out a section so that there is no pressure on the lip of the inverted casserole. Turn the base as usual. If you want to fit a lid, make one in the same way as you did for Casserole A. ▷

Making the handle

1 Throw a hollow handle for this pouring casserole. Centre 0.5kg (1lb) of clay and raise it into a narrow pillar. Plumb down through the centre to the wheelhead and raise the cylinder, keeping a flared base. ◁

2 Gradually close the walls in with successive lifts, but do not close the handle over entirely; there should be a hole at its end. ▷

3 Shape the handle so that it is comfortable to grip, remembering that oven gloves will probably be worn when lifting the casserole. Use a throwing rib to compress the clay. Trim any waste clay from the base.

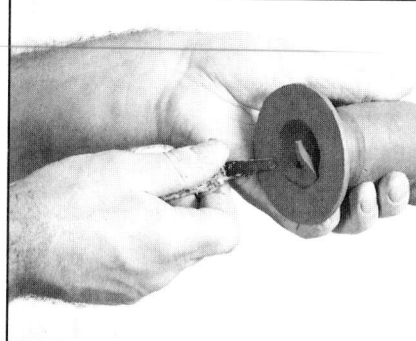

4 Once it has dried to leather hard, trim away any unwanted thickness from the inner edge and the base of the handle using a sharp knife.

6 Score the area of the casserole where the handle is to go, apply slurry and press the handle in place. Smooth the flared base into the clay wall.

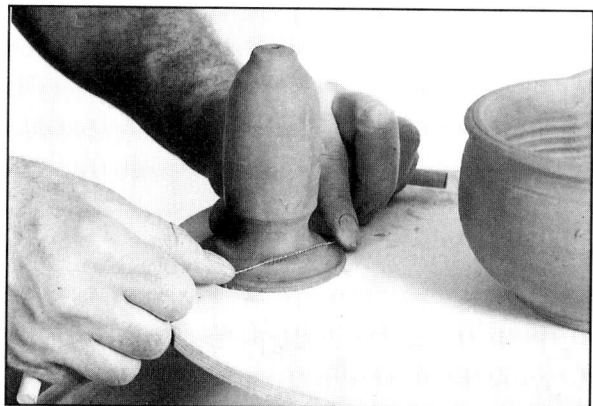

5 Slice away the clay from the flared base of the handle at a slight angle so that it will fit flush against the side of the casserole.

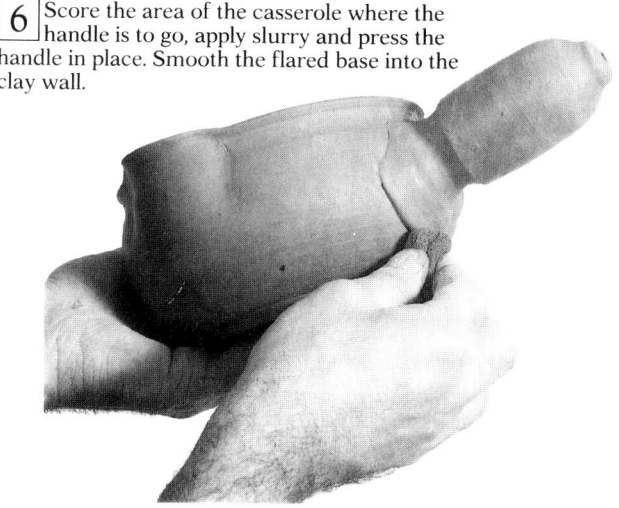

Casseroles

Functional ware used in connection with food must have
glazes that are easily cleaned. Although many clays are
"oven-proof" when fired, far fewer will withstand being
heated directly on a domestic cooker without cracking.

Dinner service

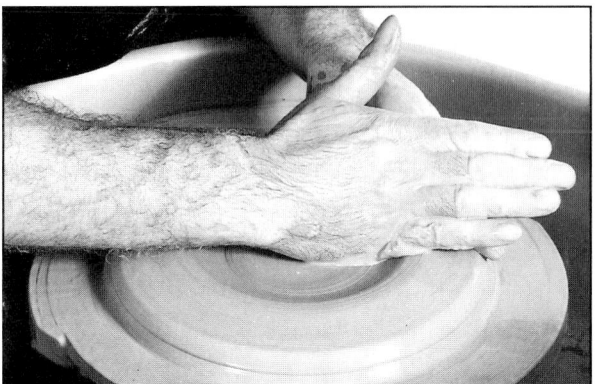

This project provides instructions for only the most basic components of a dinner service. You can adapt the tableware projects described elsewhere in the book to supplement the dinner plates and sauce boat and create a matching set.

1 For each plate, centre 2kg (4lbs) of clay. Spread the clay across the wheelhead and using the outside edge of your palm, open the clay into a very shallow plate. Keep the clay wet and use your fingers to continue shaping the plate. △

2 The plates will shrink when they are fired, so throw them to a wider diameter than that you actually require. Slightly compress the rim to give the plate a good firm edge.

3 Use a rib to smooth out the surface of the plate. Trim any excess clay away from the base, but do not take off too much because the edge of the plate might droop. Release the plate from the surface of the wheelhead with a wire.

4 When the plates are leather hard you can trim them. Invert a plate on the wheel and secure it with clay pellets. Turn the base, remembering that the plate is not particularly thick and not to pare away too much. Trim the outer edge. The larger plates will need a double footring, like the hors d'oeuvres tray (*see p55*). △

Making a serving plate

1 Make a large plate in the usual way. When it has dried to leather hard, slice two shallow eliptical shapes from opposite sides of the rim, leaving enough of the rim intact to prevent food sliding off the server. Smooth the shape off with a damp sponge. ◁

Making the sauce boat

1 Centre 0.6kg (1¼lbs) of well-prepared clay and throw a small, deep bowl. Collar the edge of it slightly to give it a full shape.

2 Gently compress the rim of the form to give it to strengthen it. Flare the edge slightly. Trim away any excess clay from the base and mop out any water.

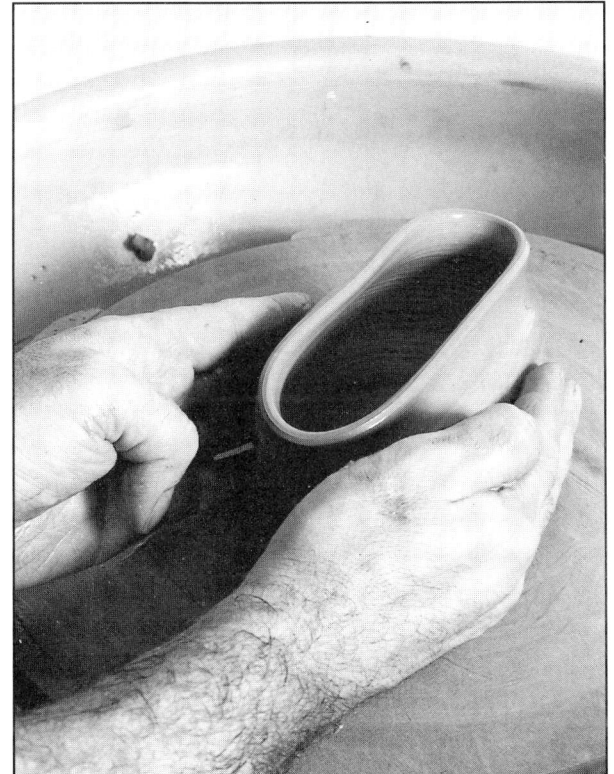

4 Form a generous pouring lip on its rim, by squeezing the rim at one end of the form very gently with your thumb and finger and easing out the clay between them. Leave the boat to dry to leather hard.

3 While the form is still soft, you can squash it gently into the traditional ovaled sauce boat shape, leaving the base circular. Take care not to close in the lips of the form too far.

Finishing touches

1 Invert and re-centre the sauce boat on the wheel, using the base area to guide you. Secure it with clay pellets. Turn the base carefully and give the form a narrow footring. ◁

2 Turn the sauce boat the right way up and with a suitable tool, mark two curved areas on either side of the rim. Cut these out with a sharp knife. These shallow dips on either side of the form accentuate its boat shape. Smooth the form off and tidy the rim. ▽

4 Invert the form on a suitable flat surface, allowing the loop of the handle to hang down while it dries so that it does not become distorted.

3 Extrude or pull a suitable handle for the sauce boat. Score the side of the rim at the back of the form and attach the handle firmly in a generous loop. Add a small coil of clay to strengthen the upper join.

Dinner set

Ilmenite oxide has been used to paint decorative bands on to
the surface of the opaque white gloss. The speckling has
been achieved by further spraying over the glazed surface,
using an old toothbrush dipped in the oxide.

Coffee set

Both styles of coffee pot described in this project are based on a jug shape with an integral or a separately thrown spout. The proportions and design of the pot you throw should be echoed by the matching mugs, jug and sugar bowl.

Style A

1 Centre 2.2kg (4½lbs) of clay and draw it up into a tapered dome. Begin to lift the walls, maintaining a good width at the base of the form. Taper the walls gradually as you raise them, keeping a thick layer of clay around the rim from which to form the internal gallery.

2 Collar the neck of the form and define the point where it emerges from the body of the form. Remove any water before you close it in too far. Trim the rim and compress it. ▷

3 Split the rim with your thumb or fingernail to make an internal gallery. Trim around the inner edge of the ledge you have made. Measure the inner diameter of the throat of the jug so that you know how large to make the lid. △

4 Trim off any excess clay. When the pot has dried to leather hard, invert it on the wheelhead. Secure it with clay pellets and turn its base. ▷

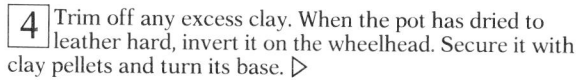

Attaching a spout

1 Throw and attach a spout in the same way as you did for the teapots (*see p61*). You can either pierce a number of pouring holes in the wall of the pot, or one large one.

2 If you opt for the latter, bevel the lower inner edge to assist the flow of liquid. The unbevelled upper edge will stop the overflow of liquid as you pour.

Making the lid

1 Centre 170g (6oz) of clay and open it out, retaining a thick outer edge. Measure the diameter before you begin to make the flange. Split the rim with your thumb nail and depress the outer side to the wheelhead to form the flange. Raise the walls of the inner section. Trim the edge of the shape with a needle. Any final shaping can be done when the clay has dried further.

2 Shape a slight spout in the inner wall so that the lid sits snugly in the neck of the pot. When the lid is leather hard, trim it to a rounded dome and define a circle at the apex of the dome. Score this area and apply slurry. Attach a small lump of clay and with the minimum of water, throw a suitable knob.

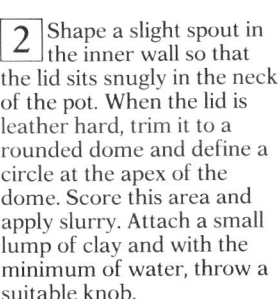

Attaching the handle

Score the areas of the coffee pot's wall where the handle is to fit. Extrude or pull a handle of a suitable length and attach it with slurry having scored its ends. Add small clay coils to both joins to reinforce them. △

Style B

1 Centre 2.7kg (5½lbs) of clay and throw a similar shaped jug to that described above. Collar the top section slightly more vigorously, but keep plenty of clay around the rim. Flare the rim slightly.

2 Trim the rim and the upper section of the jug, leaving a bulge in the neck from which to spring a handle. Remove any water from within the form.

3 Smooth the rim with a sponge and flatten and compress it. Form an internal gallery, supporting the outside of the shape. Trim any excess clay from the base. Raise an area of the rim from which to form the pouring lip.

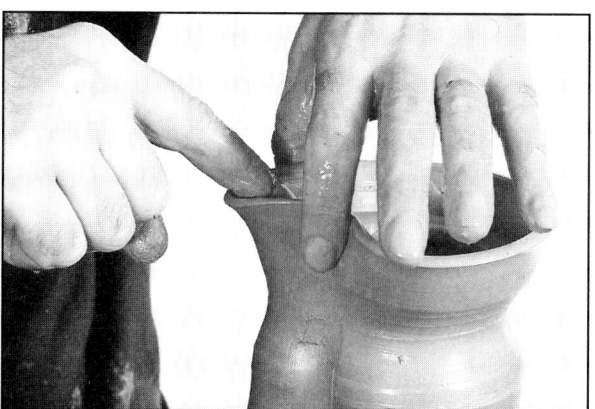

4 Smooth the edge of the internal gallery into the lip area. Using a long throwing rib, tease out the front section of the jug to form a long pouring channel. Shape the edge of the pouring lip with your fingers. △

5 Squeeze the neck of the jug to form an inner circle for the lid to sit in. When the pot has dried to leather hard, turn its base, cushioning its rim on a coil of clay to protect its spout. ▷

Attaching a handle

Make an identical lid to that described for style A, *(p86)* and attach an identical handle. Add a small piece of clay to the top of the handle and work it into the clay. Extend this to add a decorative flourish to the handle.

Decorating the pot

Decorate the body of the pot by incising lines into its surface. These cut lines produce very interesting effects when the pot is glazed. Invert the pot so that the handle hangs down as it dries.

Making the mugs

1 The mugs should all reflect the shape of the coffee pot. For each mug, centre 0.6kg (1¼lbs) of clay and throw a tapered cylinder with a flared rim.

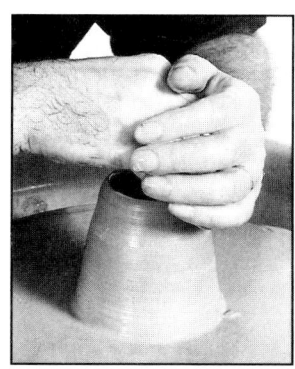

2 Create a bulge in the wall of the mug at a point about a third of the way down. A handle will be attached at this point. Remove any water from the form and trim the base.

3 When the mug has dried to leather hard, invert it on the wheelhead and turn the base. Attach a handle that reflects the shape and design of the coffee pot's handle.

Making the jug

1 Centre 0.7kg (1½lbs) of clay and throw a shape similar to that described in making the mugs, but slightly larger. Leave a thickened rim from which to make the pouring lip.

2 Raise a small section of the rim and form a spout. Indent a pouring channel inside the jug and squeeze the lip area with your fingers. When it is leather hard, invert the jug, on a coil of clay, and turn its base.

3 Attach the handle in the same way as you attached the mug's. Again, it is important from the point of view of making a set that the curve and decorative design of the handle is similar for all the components.

Making the sugar bowl

1 Centre 0.6kg (1¼lbs) of clay and spread it into a shallow domed shape. Open the clay but still maintain the same basic shape and keep the raising of the wall to an absolute minimum.

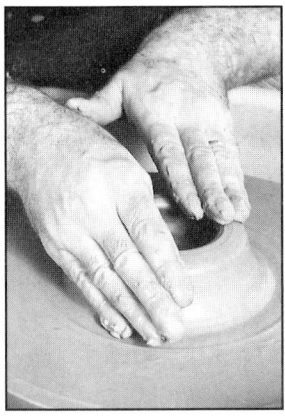

2 Gently flare the rim and form a ridge at a point a third of the way down the wall. The bowl does not need a handle but this feature makes the bowl part of the set. Remove any water from inside the form and trim its base.

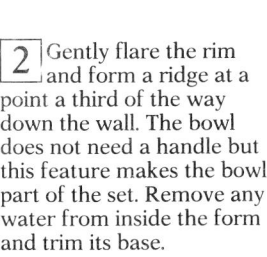

3 When the bowl has dried to leather hard, invert it on the wheelhead. Secure it with clay pellets and carefully turn its base.

Coffee set

Careful glazing of any set will help to unify all its different components. Although a semi-matt oatmeal glaze was used on these pieces, a shiny glaze has been used on the rims of the mugs so that they are pleasant to drink from.

Carafe and goblet sets

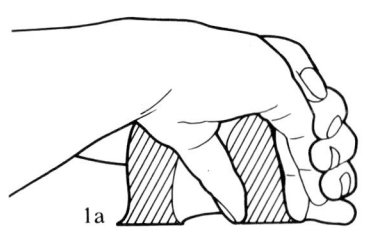

1a

Goblet A

1 Centre 0.7kg (1½lbs) of clay and form a narrow cone shape. Push your thumb through the clay right down to the wheelhead and draw the clay up in a hollow column.

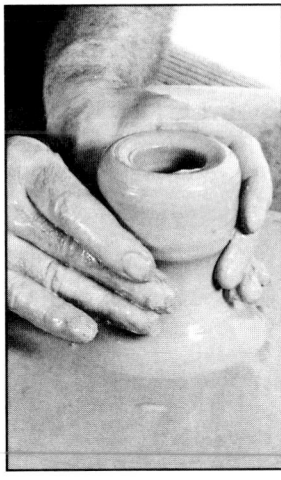

Throwing a goblet will always present the potter with the problem of maintaining stability. Leaving aside the method whereby the cup and the stem are made separately and then joined together when leather hard, the two methods described here provide a logical solution to the problem of persuading a narrow stem of clay to support a larger cup.

2 Begin to create a conical shape, collaring after each lift. Swell a cup shape and sit back from the wheel to check its proportions. Shape the walls further and refine the rim. Collar the stem just below the swell of the cup. ▷

3 Continue to refine the shape of the goblet by throwing, and by trimming away the wet clay around the stem. When the goblet has dried to leather hard, trim the inner and outer edges of the base ring so that it will sit steadily.

4 To seal the goblet, cut out a small circle from a piece of flattened clay and attach it inside the goblet at the point where the swell of the cup joins the stem. Score the areas to be joined and apply slurry. Smooth the join over.

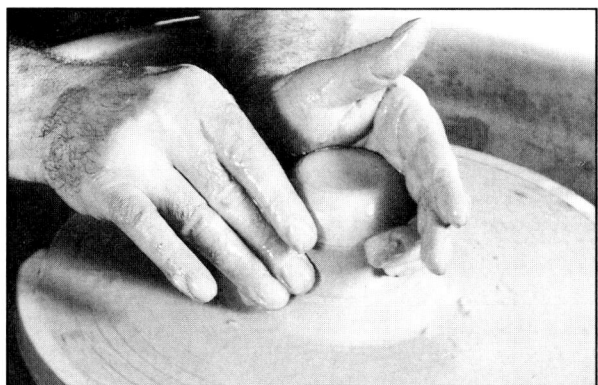

2 Continue to narrow the column until it is about 8.75cm (3½in) high. Begin to flare out a cup shape in the upper section by inserting your thumb to a depth of about 3.75cm (1½in).

Goblet B

1 To make this style of goblet, centre the clay and draw up a narrow cone. Lifting your hands away from the wheelhead, apply pressure at a point 2cm (¾in) above the base. Keep the wheel rotating at an even speed. △

4 Mop out any water from inside the cup. Raise the cup by collaring the stem of the goblet to thin it down. If you wish, you can develop a knuckle midway up the stem, (*see "Making a set"* p.33). ◁

3 Open and raise this section, ensuring that the cup you form has a good solid column of clay to support it. Check the evenness of the cup's curve by leaning back away from the wheel. Refine it as you wish.

5 As the stem narrows, support the cup with your left hand. Further shaping can then take place without upsetting the balance of the goblet. Trim away any excess clay and shape the base of the goblet with a trimming tool.

The principle behind making any set is to maintain a unity of design through each component. These carafes are designed to echo the different styles of the goblets described in this project.

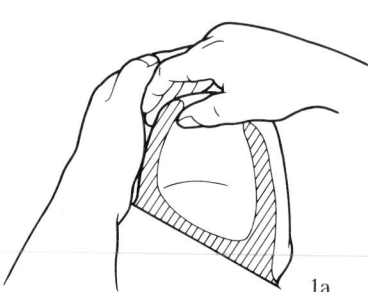

1a

Style A

1 Begin with 2.5kg (5lbs) of clay centred and flared out at the base. As you begin to raise the clay, maintain the lines of the initial conical profile by tapering as you lift.

2 As the form grows, define the point where the neck will emerge by collaring gently.

3a

3 Keep the upper cylindrical section relatively wide as you finish the lower half of the carafe. Mop out any water inside the form with a sponge.

4 Begin to collar the upper section fairly vigorously bearing in mind that you are aiming to form a narrow neck. Keep your eye on the point where the neck section begins.

6 Even off the walls of the base section with a throwing rib, supporting the neck as you go. Shape area where the swell of the base narrows into the neck.

5 As the upper portion narrows down, the walls will thicken providing you with plenty of clay from which to throw the neck of the form. Lift the narrowed shape smoothly and evenly and keep the whole form steadied.

8 Thin the rim at one point with your thumb and forefinger to increase the workable area from which to create a spout. Hold the edge of this area of the rim with two fingers and tease out a spout.

7 Taper the neck of the carafe and begin to open the rim out to form a flared edge. Tidy off any ragged edges around the rim. When the carafe has dried to leather hard, you can attach a handle if you wish (*see "Handles", p29*).

Style B

1 Centre 2.5kg (5lbs) of clay. Draw the clay in at the base, rather than flaring it out. This establishes the basic form of the carafe. From the very first lift, you should try to encourage the development of a spherical base section by pulling up, and simultaneously pushing outwards.

2 Begin to collar the shape bringing the clay up from the base. Mop out any water. Keep the base steady and begin to close in the upper portion of the form, narrowing the neck while still maintaining the swell of the base. ◁

3 Compressing a ridge at the point where the neck emerges from the base will help to prevent the base sagging as you work on the upper section, lifting and tapering the neck. Trim the rim off with a pin and smooth it down with a sponge.

4 Define the lip of the carafe using a rib and pass the rib down the neck to even and smooth the clay surface. Trim away any excess clay at the base. If you wish you can attach a slender handle once the carafe has dried to leather hard (*see "Handles", p29*).

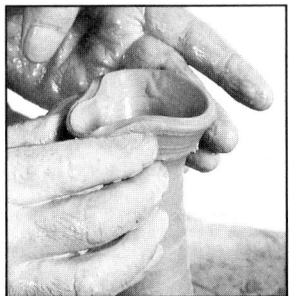

5 Thin the rim at one point with your thumb and forefinger to form the area from which to make a spout. Hold the edge of the rim with two fingers and ease out a spout.

Carafes and goblets

A simple brushed design can be achieved with loosely
applied brushstrokes to produce an attractive, informal set.
If you are worried that your design might look untidy, brush
it on a glaze that will run and blur during firing.

Lamp base

The technique involved in this project is that of constructing a large composite form. It can of course be adapted to make any form that you feel is too large for you to throw as one piece. An interesting decorative motif, such as the one illustrated, will add a new perspective to this lamp base and make it a unique and personal possession.

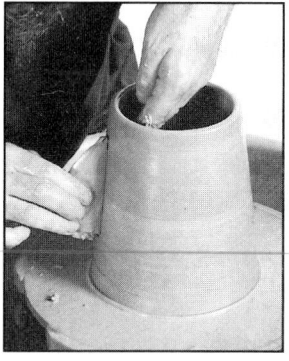

2 Define the shape of the cylinder and compress its walls with a trimming tool or rib. Trim the rim with a needle and compress it. Remove any water from the form.

1 Centre 2.5kg (5lbs) of clay. The lamp will be more stable if its base is broader than its upper section, so bear this in mind as you start to throw. Raise and taper the walls gently with successive lifts.

3 With calipers measure the outer diameter of the rim. This measurement is crucially important because it will dictate the width of the upper section of the lamp base.

4 Decorate the base of the form with clay roulettes. You can make these by impressing a texture into discs of plastic clay and then biscuit-firing them. They have holes in their centres through which a piece of wire is threaded so that these "wheels" can be rolled over the surface of a pot to produce a decorative imprint. It is best to leave the clay form until it has stiffened before decorating it, because the impressed pattern will show up more clearly.

Making the upper section

1 Centre 2.5kg (5kg) of clay and open it out to the correct diameter, right down to the wheelhead. The shape of the cylinder you throw is a matter of personal preference – you can extend it as a straight form or develop a swell in the walls.

2 To give the form a swell at its base, ease the clay out smoothly from a point about 1cm ($\frac{2}{5}$in) above the level of the wheelhead, ensuring that you do not alter the width. ▷

3 Whichever method you choose, collar the upper section of the cylinder to form a neck into which a bulb fitting can be inserted. Smooth off the rim with a sponge and trim away any excess clay from the base.

4 Check the outer base diameter using calipers and adjust it using a trimming tool if it is too wide to fit on to the neck of the lower section.

5 You can either leave the top section of the lamp plain, or decorate it to match the lower section. An interesting way to echo the design would be to decorate the clay within a band area outlined around the form.

6 Join the two sections when they have stiffened. Score the top rim of the lower section and the adjoining rim of the upper. Apply slurry to the edge of the lower section and press the pieces together. Smooth and seal the join. Running a decorated clay roulette around the join will disguise it very well. ◁

7 Using a piercing tool, gently make a hole in the wall of the lamp base at a point near its base. This allows the electric cable to be attached. If the opening at the top of the lamp base is too large for a standard light fitting, you can fit a wide cork inside it, cut specifically to hold the fitting. △

Lamp base

Iron oxide was rubbed into the richly textured surface of the
lamp base to colour it without obscuring the relief. The top
section was then dipped in an opaque white glaze. The iron
oxide altered the colour of the glaze.

Candle holders

The essence of any candle holder is the siting of the candle, and its capacity to contain the molten wax. The first of these candle holders is made to a traditional portable design, while the second is more like a night light. Both involve the same technique.

Style A

1 Centre 1.2kg (2½lbs) of clay into a low dome. Begin to open the clay using both your forefingers, pressing into the dome at a point, about 2.5cm (1in) from its centre. This causes a solid pillar of clay to emerge in the exact centre of the form. ▷

2 Raise the outer walls with one finger, forming a trough-like collar around the central pillar of clay. Shape the rim of this collar by compressing it and gently easing the outer edge of it over your fingers. △

3 Hollow out the clay pillar by plumbing into it with your finger. Shape the wall to match the thickness of the outer wall. Once the basic candle siting has emerged, you can modify its height and design. It is a good idea to extend the candle holder above the level of the outer wall.

5 Score the flattened area of the form. Score the end of the handle, apply slurry and press it into place. Ensure that the loop of the handle provides a comfortable grip. Invert the candle holder so that the handle loop does not droop during drying.

4 Remove any water from the shape and trim any excess clay away from the base. Gently flatten one side of the circular form to create a surface on which to attach a widely looped handle. Leave the form to dry to leather hard.

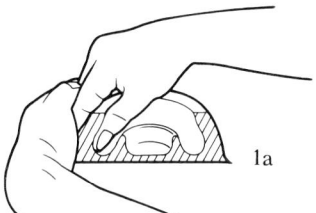

1a

Style B

1 Centre 2.5kg (3lbs) of clay and raise it into a high, narrow dome. Push down through the clay at the apex of the dome with your thumb, to a depth of about 2.5cm (1in).

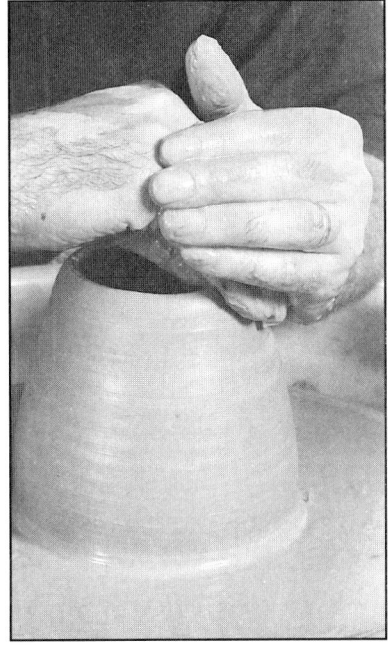

2 Continue to exert pressure, but push out at an angle towards the outer edge of the base, thus forming a central peak within the wide cone shape. Once the peak is formed, impress your finger into its top, forming an open cuff in which to stand a candle.

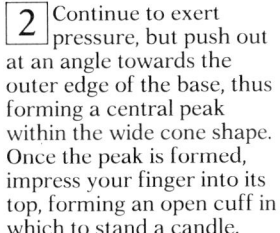

3 Begin to raise the outer walls around the central candle siting, drawing the mass of clay up from the base. Collar the walls slightly as you lift them to maintain a beehive shape.

4 Collar the clay quite firmly to emphasize the swell of the walls above the candle cuff and increase the thickness of clay around the rim from which to extend the form.

5 Finalize the lifting of the outer wall and begin to close the rim inwards to form a narrowed lip. Trim off the rim of the form with a needle.

6 Add definition and strength to the walls of the shape by compressing it with a throwing rib. Impress a slight ledge into the upper section so that the ultimate shape of the candle holder resembles a night light. Trim away any excess clay from the base.

8 Using a pin, cut through the wall of the form following the guideline of the shape you have drawn and remove the segment of clay. Be careful not to cut out your shape at a point too near the base, where the clay is thick. Tidy off the edges of the hole and smooth the shape with a sponge.

7 When the form has dried to leather hard, mark the area you will cut out on the side of it. Any shape is perfectly acceptable – the hole simply has to be large enough to allow the candle light to shine out.

Candle holders

A basic matt white glaze was used on both these candle holders. A second darker glaze was then poured over to break up the overall pale colour and give the shapes a further dimension.

Pot Pourri

Literally translated, "pot pourri" means rotten pot which graphically describes the appearance of this pierced pot. The fragrances of the dried flowers and scented herbs with which it is filled permeate the atmosphere via these holes. This particular design allows the pot to be hung or free-standing.

Making the base

1 Centre 2kg (4lbs) of clay and draw it up into a rounded shape. As you raise the walls, ensure that there is plenty of clay around the rim from which to make the internal ledge. ◁

2 Spread the thickness of clay at the rim over the top of your left forefinger, held within the pot. The clay at the rim of the pot will flatten and extend inwards to form a smooth ledge. △

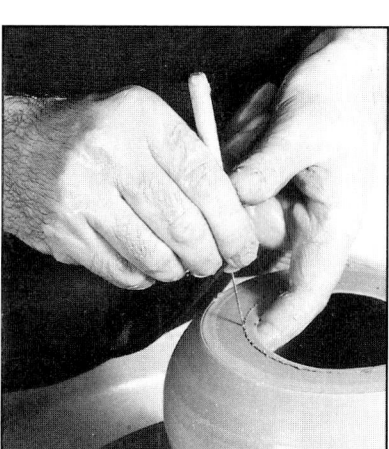

3 Smooth off and compress the outside of the pot with a rib and tidy the rim. Trim away any excess clay from the edge of the ledge with a needle and remove any water from within the form. △

4 Measure the outer diameter of the rim with a pair of calipers so that you know how wide to make the top.

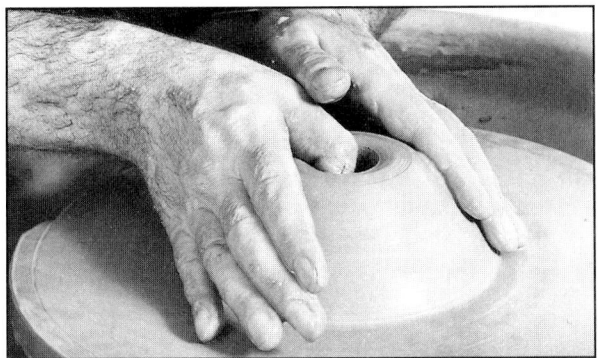

Making the top

1 Centre 1.2kg (2½lbs) of well-prepared clay and form it into a shallow dome. Open it out down to the wheelhead to the correct diameter, pushing outwards with your thumb. △

2 Lift the wall, forming the two ledges immediately. Collar the clay briefly just above the base. Allow the clay to open and then close in above this second ridge. ◁

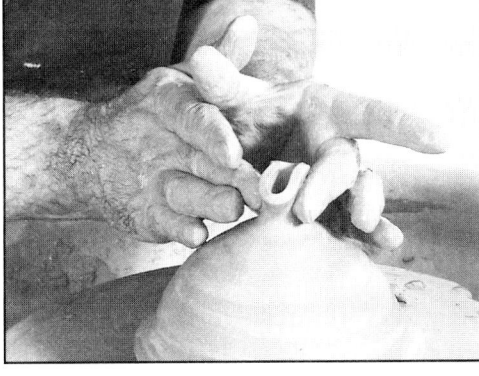

4 Flatten the upper spout into a fan shape. Slice through the base with a cutting wire to release the clay from the wheelhead. △

3 Swell the walls of the form to give a good rounded shape. Close in the top section, finishing the edge off into a short neck. Trim the top and the base of the form. △

5 When the lid has dried to leather hard, invert it in a suitable chuck on the wheelhead and trim its underside. Trim the lower ledge to correspond with the main body width. ▷

The finishing touches

1 When the base has dried to leather hard, invert and centre it on the wheelhead. If you want to hang the pot, you can trim the base completely round; if you want to keep your options open, trim the base flat so that you can stand or hang it. Trim the two pieces so that they share the same outer diameter.

2 Cut out two sections from the rim of the bottom half, using guidelines measured with a ruler.

3 Cut out two sections from the upper half, creating ledges that are the same size as the cut-out areas of the bottom half. Use the same measurement guidelines to do this. Trim these projecting ledges so that they slot easily into the gaps in the lower rim.

4 With a piercing tool, make several holes in the bottom half, creating as simple or as elaborate a design as you wish. If you want to suspend the pot, pierce a hole in the top of the lid.

Pot pourri

The many decorative holes of the pot have been highlighted with cobalt oxide. The oxide was brushed over a matt white glaze to produce this soft blue colour. The colours of the pot pourri petals add to the decorative scheme of the form.

Mirror frame

A mirror or indeed a picture frame can be made with equal ease by following this simple method. The frame need not be circular: it can be shaped into an oval or a square. If you do change the shape of the form, you should trim it while it is pliable.

1 Centre about 1kg (2lbs) of clay and flatten it into a shallow dome. With your thumb, push down through the clay to the wheelhead. Open the clay out by pushing with both thumbs in opposite directions. As you widen the ring of clay, press down on to the surface of the clay with the base of your thumbs to prevent it splitting.

2 Indent the surface of the ring with your finger. Smooth the form over and trim its inner and outer edges. There are many different ways of decorating the frame. You could apply a light-coloured slip and draw on a darker design with a slip trailer.

3 You could roll a long coil of clay and make a pattern by pressing it into the indent of the frame. Clay pellets can also be added. You could use different colour clays, or different coloured slips. A clay roulette could be used to impress a pattern into the surface of the frame. Use a roller to flatten the pattern you have chosen to create.

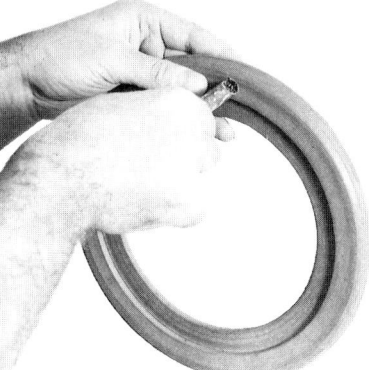

4 When the frame has dried to leather hard, invert it on the wheelhead and secure it with clay pellets. Trim away any ragged edges and form an inner ledge, deep enough for the mirror or the picture, backing card and glass.

5 To hang the frame, pierce a hole at a suitable point on the perimeter of the frame, or attach a coil of clay in a small loop.

Mirror or picture frame

Iron oxide was brushed onto the surface of the frame and then wiped off the raised surface. A shiny glaze was brushed over its inner and outer edges to produce further textural contrasts.

Self-draining plant pot

Most people have their own favourite houseplants and like to keep them in attractive containers. This self-draining plant pot combines good looks with utility. It is sturdy, well-balanced and its drainage holes enable you to plant directly into it.

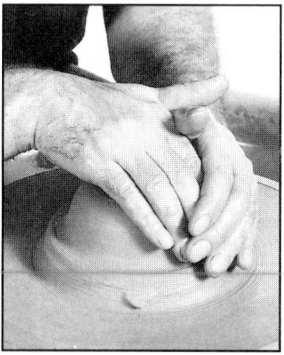

1 Centre 2kg (4lbs) of well-prepared clay and form it into a full dome. Once the clay is centred, move your hands so that you are applying pressure at a point 1.8cm (³⁄₄in) above the level of the wheelhead.

2 As pressure is applied a thick basal collar of clay will emerge – this will be used to form the drainage tray. Supporting the clay with your palms, begin to plumb into the dome with your thumbs.

3 Open out the main body of clay, steering clear of the clay collar at its base. Gradually lift the wall, shaping it so that it flares gently outwards with successive lifts.

4 Refine the edge of the rim with your fingertips, easing it up and out over the fingers of your supporting hand. Link up your hands for extra support. △

5 Finalize the shaping of the pot's rim by pushing the clay out against a rubber kidney and simultaneously indenting the body of the pot just below the rim. ▷

6 To make the drainage tray, impress the clay collar at the base of the pot using your right forefinger. Support your right hand with your left and ensure that you keep the pressure exerted by keeping your forefinger steady. △

7 Extend the wall to a suitable height, shaping its edge with your fingers to reflect the shape of the rim of the pot. Be careful not to distort the walls of the pot. ▷

8 Any refining of the shape of the drainage tray can be undertaken when you trim the base of the form to remove excess clay. Hold the trimming tool steadily against the side of the tray's wall as you pare the clay away.

9 Remove any water from inside the pot and the drainage tray using a small sponge. Smooth down the rim with a damp sponge or a strip of chamois leather.

Finishing touches

1 Once the pot has dried to leather hard, turn its base. Because of the raised internal pot shape, the base is relatively thick and quite a large amount of clay can be pared away. △

2 Using a piercing tool, make four drainage holes at the base of the pot. Hold the tool at an angle to the wall of the pot to ensure that the holes made allow water to drain away easily. ◁

Self-draining plant pot

Glazes of a fairly neutral colour are the best choice for decorating a plant pot, so that there is no risk of the pot detracting from the beauty of the species of plant it contains.

Puzzle jug

The puzzle jug is a traditional vessel that has re-emerged recently as a popular novelty. Puzzle jugs are traditionally associated with bucolic celebrations, where they provided party-goers with an amusing test of skill. Nowadays, that same test has lost none of its appeal; nor has the attractive design of the jug.

1a
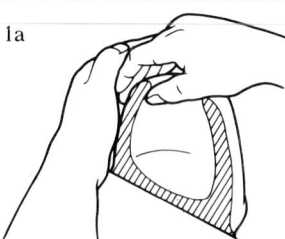

1 Centre 1.5kg (3lbs) of well-prepared clay. Throw a basic jug shape, swelling the clay out to form a belly and collaring for a neck. As you lift the walls of the form, keep in mind the shape you are aiming for. △

2 When you reach the rim, keep the clay fairly thick as you will need plenty of scope to successfully create the special puzzle rim. Trim the rim with a needle and begin to form the looped rim.

3 Flare out the rim until it is almost flat, supporting its underside with your left forefinger. Continue to maintain this support and start to exert pressure downwards with your right forefinger so that the clay begins to curl round towards the neck of the jug. △

4 When the rim has curved round to meet the wall of the jug, seal the join with a modelling tool. Take out any water and trim around the base. ▷

Making the handle

1 The handle is made by cutting a suitable length from a hollow ring of clay. Centre 0.5kg (1lb) of clay. Push your thumb down through the clay to meet the surface of the wheelhead and open it out as you would if you were making a shallow dish.

3 Before you close the form completely, make a hole in the inner wall to allow the escape of any air. Seal the ring with a trimming tool. Remove any clay around the inner and outer edges of the ring with a trimming tool to give it a smooth, rounded shape. Leave the ring to stiffen before cutting a handle. ▽

2 Open out the form to create a slim ring of clay. Support the sides of the ring with your left hand and using your right forefinger, impress a ridge into the clay. The ring will gradually divide and a shallow cuff will emerge. Neaten the edges of the cuff with your fingertips. Start to extend the outer wall gently, encouraging the clay to curve towards the inner wall. When the clay walls have met, use your fingers to seal the two edges together.

Making the spouts

1 Throw the spouts using a technique known as "stack-throwing", where several small forms are thrown from the top of a clay stack. Centre a good-sized lump of clay, and lift it into a cone. Push your fingertip down into the clay to a depth that corresponds to the height of the spouts. Shape this indented section into a thick-lipped spout.

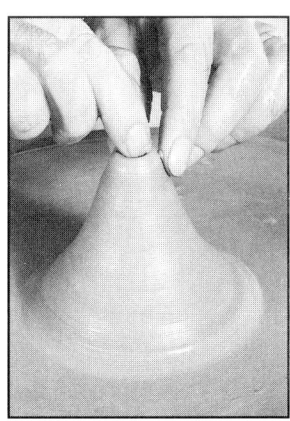

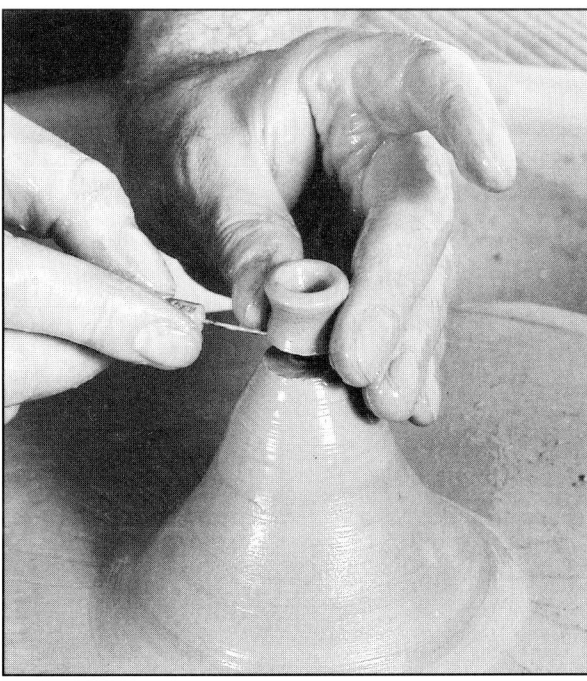

2 Cut off the spout section using a needle. The segment you remove from the clay should be completely hollow. Throw several spouts of the same general size.

The finishing touches

1 Turn the base of the jug when it is leather hard. Using a piercing tool, make several holes around the neck section of the jug. The pattern of holes can be as simple or elaborate as you wish. Smooth the edges when dry.

2 Shape a section of the handle to fit the jug. Pierce one hole in the jug at a point 2–3cm (3/4–1 1/4 in) up from the base, another in the rim directly above this hole, and a third in the upper curve of the handle itself. Blow down the handle to check that it is not blocked. Score around the two holes in the jug and the cut surfaces of the handle. Attach the handle to the jug with slurry, ensuring that the holes in the rim and at the base of the jug are lined up with the hollow handle. Smooth the joins over, supporting the jug with your other hand.

4 Attach all the other spouts you have made in the same way, but without making a hole in the rim of the jug. Paint the body of the jug with a coloured slip so that you can scratch a traditional puzzle jug verse on to the jug's surface when the slip dries.

3 Make a genuine hole for a spout in the rim of the jug opposite the handle. Flatten the base of the spout out a little. Score the surface of the rim around the spout hole, and the flattened surface of the spout. Attach the spout to the rim with slurry, being careful not to clog the hole. △

5 This is a process known as "sgraffito". The contrasting colour of the clay beneath the slip brings a touch of life to the jug, and you can choose the words you want to inscribe to suit any special occasion. Traditional verses, however, do seem to be more appropriate.

Puzzle jugs

Here are two traditional verses to inscribe on puzzle jugs. A simple transparent glaze has been used to ensure that the verses remain legible.

Here gentlemen come try your skill.
I'll hold a wager if you will
That you can't drink this liqor all.
Without you spill or let some fall.

Within this jug there be good liqor,
Fit for parson or for vicar.
But to drink and not to spill
Will try the utmost of your skill.

Bird and animal forms

All these little creatures are thrown following a very similar basic technique which readily adapts itself to produce a variety of very different shapes. There is plenty of scope for inventing your own favourites, developing your own additions from these initial ideas and incorporating your own decorative innovations.

Gull

1 Centre 0.8kg (1¾lbs) of clay. Throw a narrow cone and as it grows collar the form in. Continue to lift the walls swelling the base of the cylinder out slightly. Take out any water from inside the shape with a sponge.

2 Collar the shape at two points to define the body, head and beak areas of the gull.

3 Taper and close the final beak section until it takes the form of a fine, elongated cone. Trim off any unevenness at its end. △

4 When the form is closed, you can modify the shape of the gull's head and body — the middle and lower sections of the form. Collar the head section until it is in proportion with the rest of the form. Trim away any excess clay from the base.

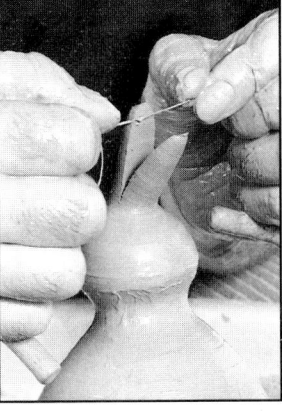

6 Stop the wheel and continue to alter the angle that the head and beak make with the gull's body. Split the beak section carefully with a taut wire and ease the two flaps this creates slightly apart to give the gull an open beak.◁

5 To give the gull a more realistic attitude, carefully shift its head section slightly off centre so that it points away from the form at a gentle angle. Lubricate the clay generously as you mould the angle.◁

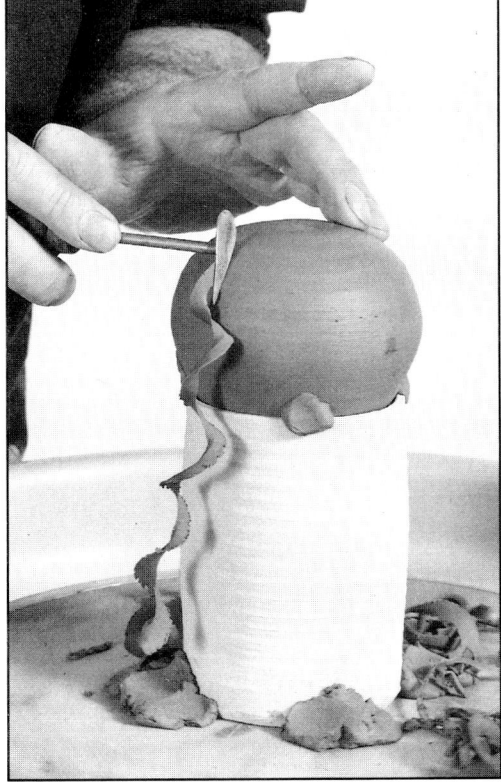

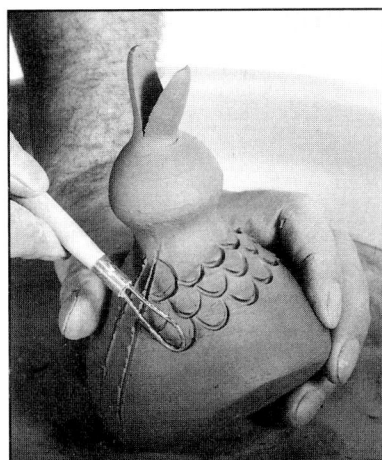

7 Use a thrown cylinder or a suitable piece of tubing for the chuck to trim the base of the gull once it is leather hard. Invert the gull into the chuck and secure it with small pellets of clay. Trim its base until it has a smooth rounded shape, then push the gull down on to a flat surface at an angle. Tap it gently until it has a steady resting base. Pierce a hole in the base to release the air pressure.

8 Add decorative "bird-like" features to the gull using a looped wire tool. Define the wing area and the plummage. Once the decoration is defined, cut into the clay to give the features some depth. Draw on the eyes with the looped wire.

Owl

1 Centre 0.8kg (1¾lbs) of clay. Throw a narrow cylinder and begin to taper it slightly. Swell the lower section of the form, but begin to narrow it at a point about two thirds of the way up the form so as to create an upper section for the owl's head.

2 Begin to collar this upper section, but ensure that you leave a large enough gap to be able to use one finger to continue to raise the form and shape the head.

3 When you are happy with the proportions of the owl, take out any water with a sponge on a stick and close the shape over. Trim away any excess clay from around the base.

4 Modify the shape further if you wish once the form is closed. Define the eye areas on the head section by pressing and rubbing gently with your fingers. Leave the shape to dry to leather hard.

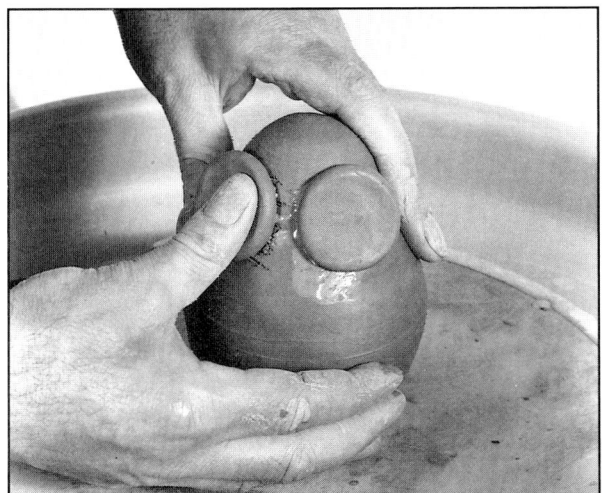

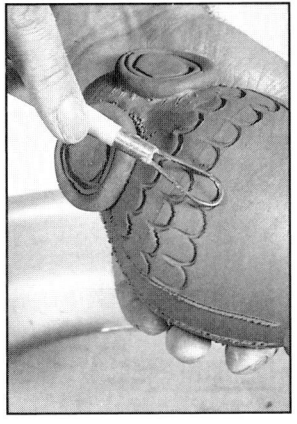

6 Impress the plummage on the owl's breast with a looped wire tool. Cut into these markings to give them an interesting texture. Brush off any excess clay.

5 Trim the base of the form in the same way you did the gull. Stand the owl upright. Make two small discs of clay from two clay balls. Score the eye areas and attack the discs with slurry. Make concentric imprints in the discs using any appropriate round object, completing the eyes with a central circle. △

7 Define the wing areas on the sides of the owl. Holding the owl firmly but carefully, score decorative feather markings down over the clay with a suitable tool.◁

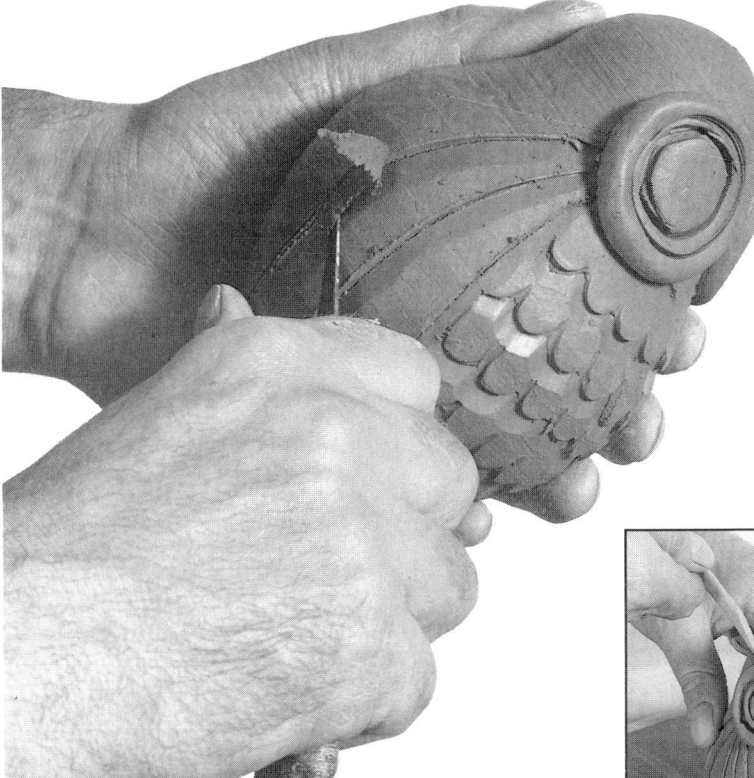

8 Fashion a small beak from a small pellet of clay and attach it with slurry. Pierce small holes into it to represent the owl's nostrils. Attach the owl's ears in the same way. Pierce the base of the form.

Hedgehog

1 Centre 0.8kg (1¾lbs) of clay and draw it into a squat dome shape. Begin to open the shape, aiming for a rounded shape as you lift the walls.

2 Collar in quite tightly at a point about one third of the way down the shape, thereby forming a narrowed upper section. Take out any water with a sponge on a stick. ▽

3 Support the lower rounded shape as you continue to narrow the emerging neck into a thin cylindrical pipe — this will eventually be the hedgehogs snout. Trim off the rim of this pipe with a pin.

4 Continue to shape the snout, adding a knuckle if you want to. Trim away any excess clay from the base. To make the hedgehog look more realistic, move the snout slightly off centre until it points out at an angle. Leave the form to dry to leather hard. Trim the base of the hedgehog and flatten it so that the hedgehog sits at an angle.

5 Pierce two eye holes in the form just above the snout and finish the eyes by drawing eyebrows with a looped wire tool. To make the hedgehog's "spines", push a lump of clay through a sieve and cut off the extruded lengths. Apply slurry to the hedgehog's back and stick the clay spines either all over it, or on the top of the hedgehog's head. If you opt for the second method, score spine-like lines on the hedgehog's body. △

Bird and animal forms

Manganese dioxide has been used to accentuate the "feathers" of the gull and the owl. Both a matt and an opaque white glaze were used for these shapes. Leaving part of a shape unglazed can be effective.

Chess set

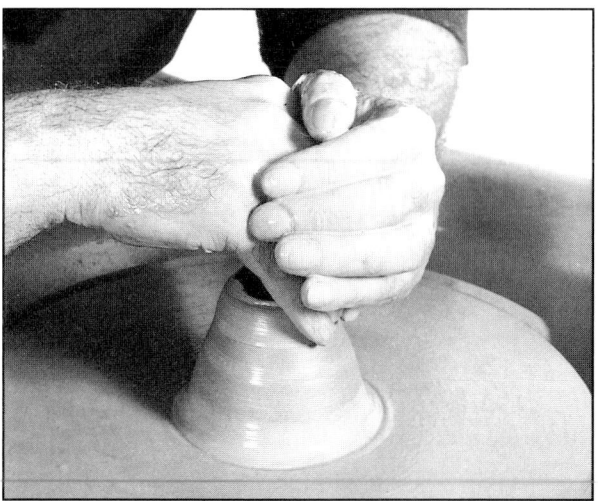

Throwing a chess set is a test of both imagination and creative skill. Choose your own decorative theme, remembering that as long as the different pieces are easily recognizable, they can all be individually characterized.

Making the pawns

1 For each pawn, centre 0.5kg (1lb) of clay. Form it into a narrow dome shape with the diameter you want the pieces to have. Plumb through the clay to the wheelhead and raise and taper the walls.

2 Roughly define the head and body areas with successive lifts. Begin to collar the shape at its rim and finally close it over entirely. Any further shaping can take place at this stage.

3 Form a small ledge around the base to help balance the shape. Trim away any excess clay and smooth the shape off. ◁

4 Measure the height and width of the form so that you have a constant sizing for all the pawns. △

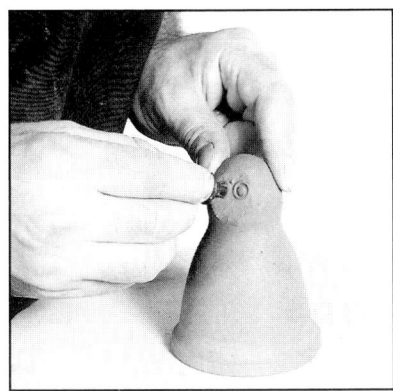

Decorating the pawns

1 When the pawns are leather hard, trim around their bases to give them a uniform silhouette. The way you characterize the pawns, or indeed any of the pieces, is of course up to you. As long as the pieces are recognizable you can decorate them exactly as you wish.

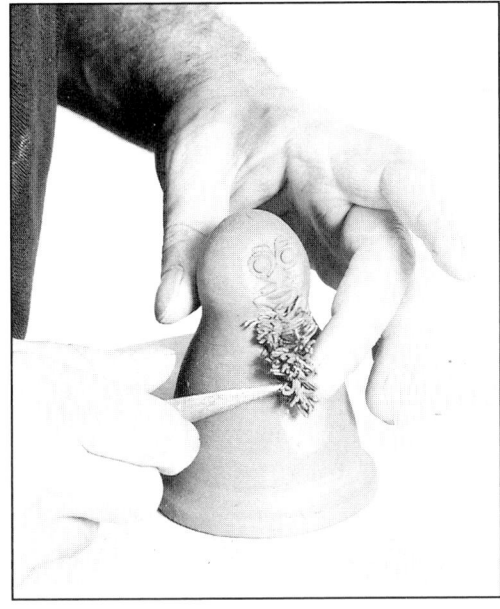

2 Slice a section off the front of the head to make a face. Paint this area with slurry and make the pawn's features by pressing small pellets of clay into place and marking the clay. Make a beard by forcing a lump of clay through a sieve to make shreds of clay, as you did for the hedgehog, *(see p124)*.

3 Attach a coil of clay around the neck of the pawn and decorate it. The arms can be made by simply shaping two small pieces of clay and attaching them with slurry to meet across the belly. Model the hands from two small balls of clay.

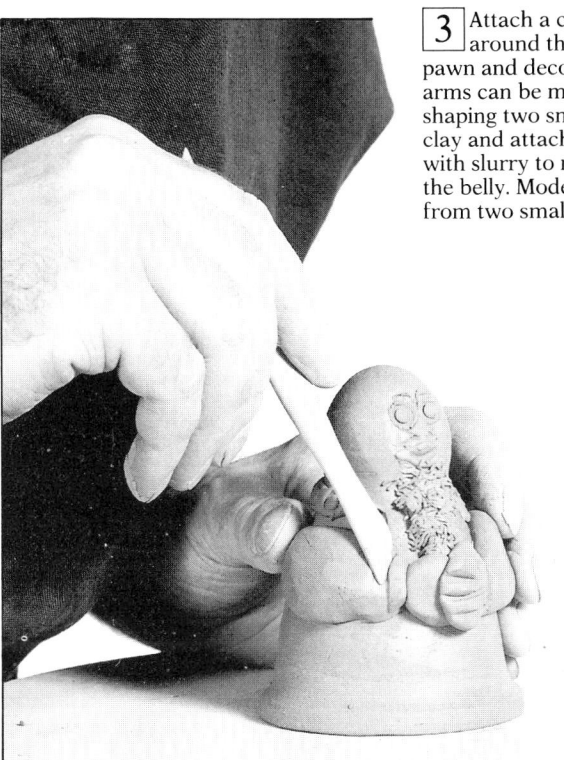

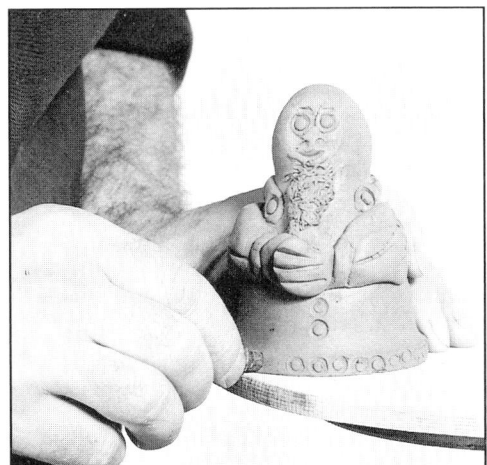

4 Indent a pattern around the base of the form with a suitable tool. Repeat the same decorative features on all the pawns to make a set.

Making the bishops and the knights

1 Both the bishop and the knight are basically the same shape and height. Centre 0.7kg (1½lbs) and throw a form following the directions described for the pawns, but make sure that it is noticeably taller.

2 Define the difference between the two pieces when you form the head and body areas. Take out any water from within the form. Collar and close its top over and finalise any shaping. Indent a ledge at the base of the form and trim away any excess clay.

Decorating the knight

1 Define the knight's armour by attaching a thin coil of clay around the "shoulders" of the form. Make his visor by attaching an eliptical loop of clay coil across his head.

2 Model a pair of arms as you did for the pawn, and attach them with slurry. Place a clay coil around his wrists and model his hands.

3 Flatten a piece of clay and cut out a long shield shape. Attach a clay coil heraldic decoration to the shield with slurry. Press the shield in place on the Knight.

Decorating the bishop

1 Slice off a section of the head to make a face. Add the details of his face and a long beard. Flatten a piece of clay and cut out two mitre shapes. Join them together and attach the mitre to the top of the bishop's head with slurry. Press a clay coil around the edge of the mitre and indent a cross into the front of it.

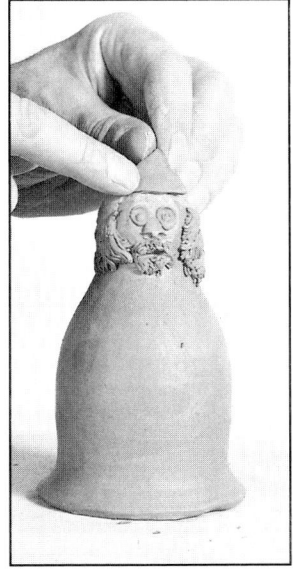

2 Model his arms and his praying hands from coils of clay. Define the edge of his cloak using a clay coil and add another coil around his neck for a collar. ▷

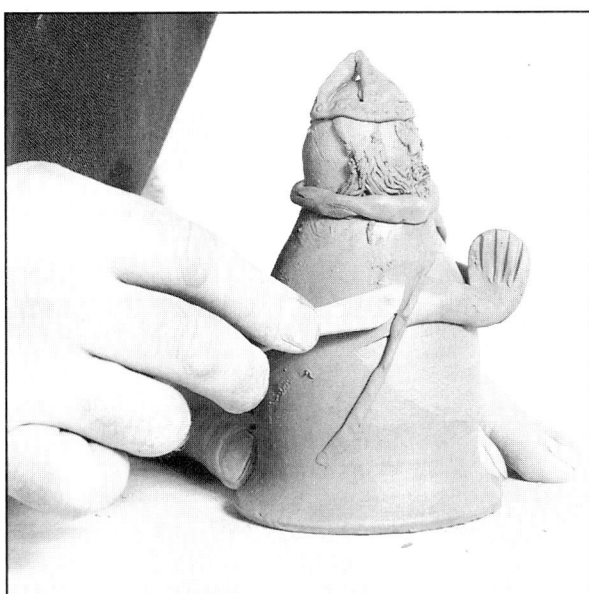

3 With a very fine coil of clay, make a rosary and attach it so that he seems to be clasping it in his hands. Decorate the edge of his cloak and gown with a suitable tool.

Making the castles

1 For each castle, centre 0.5kg (1lb) of clay and raise a straight sided cylinder. The castles should be taller than the pawns.

2 Flare the shape slightly and form a narrow ridge around the rim from which to cut the crenelations. Form another ridge around the base to echo the upper ridge. Trim away the excess clay from around the base and take out any water from within the form.

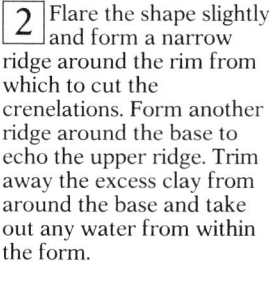

3 When the form is leather hard, turn the base if necessary. To make the crenelations, mark out the clay to be removed and carefully cut out the clay pieces, using a sharp knife. Smooth the edges down.

4 Decorate the walls of the castle with thin coils of clay, attached with slurry and smoothed into the body of the form, or left as a relief.

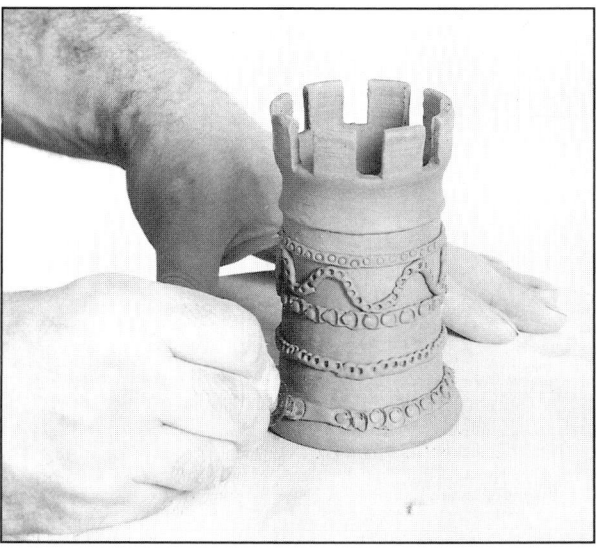

5 How you shape these coils is up to you. With a suitable implement you can apply textures and specific patterns to give the clay an interesting texture.

2 Define four body areas. Collar the cylinder in the areas corresponding to her waist, her neck and the top of her head. The uppermost section will be her crown, so ensure that it is evenly flared. Trim the edge of her crown and indent a ledge around the base. When the form is leather hard you can decorate it.

Making the queens

1 Both kings and queens are made in the same way, with the shaping of their bodies serving to distinguish between them. Centre 1kg (2lbs) of clay to make the queen. Throw a straight-sided cylinder that tapers towards its rim.

3 Define the crown area with a knife. Slice off a section of clay from the head area to form a face. Apply slurry to the face and attach clay pellets to make the Queen's eyes and nose. Define her eyebrows, eyes and mouth with a suitable tool. Push a lump of clay through a sieve to make her hair. Attach the hair just beneath her crown.

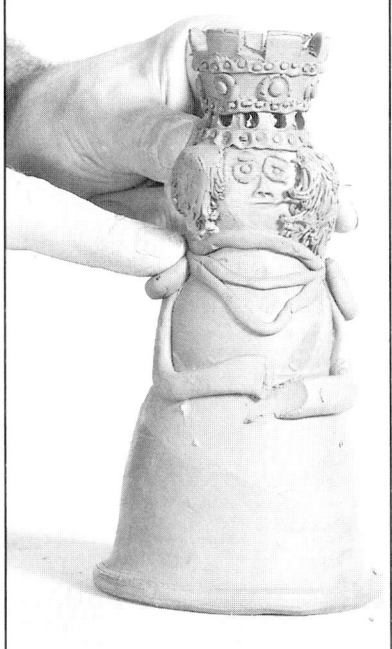

4 Decorate her crown in any way you think appropriate — piercing holes and adding coils and pellets of clay. Cut out an interesting design from the rim of the crown. Model a pair of arms from lengths of clay.

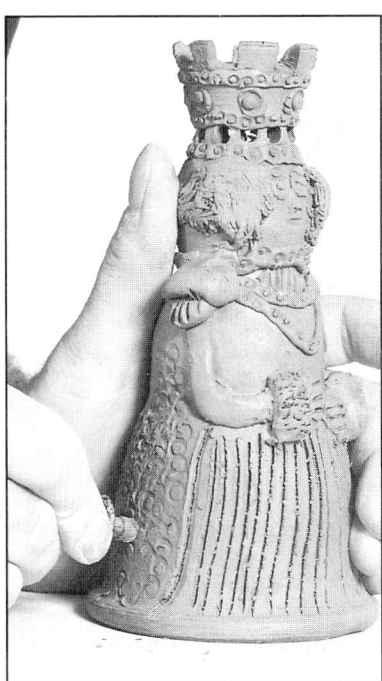

5 Use clay coils to define the shape and detail of her clothes. Model some shoulder ruffles and cuffs around her wrists. Fashion her hands from clay. Score and impress her "skirt" to give it the look of fabric.

Making the kings

1 Centre 1.1kg (2¼lbs). Extend the height of the cylinder beyond the height of the queen.

2 Instead of collaring three times to shape the piece only collar to define his head and his crown — the King has a portly silhouette.

3 Trim the edge of the crown carefully with a needle and indent a smooth decorative ledge around the base using a throwing rib

Decorating the kings

1 When the form is leather hard, define the crown area with a knife. Make the king's face and a majestic beard. Attach a thick coil of clay around the back of his neck to give the appearance of a fur collar.

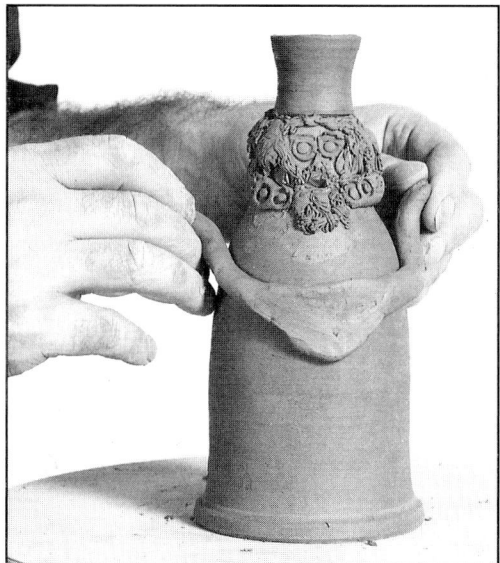

2 Make some hair in the usual way and attach it beneath his crown. Attach two clay coils to the sides of his body for arms and flatten them into sleeves. Use another clay coil to define the edge of his cloak, leading from his neck down and around his back.

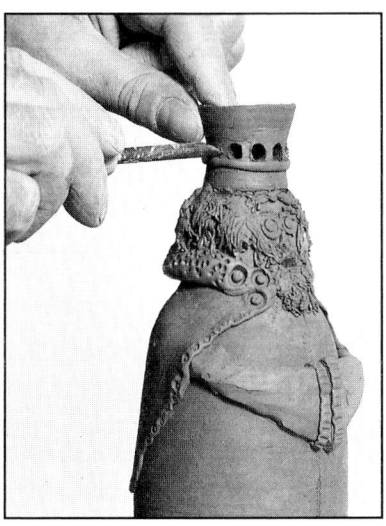

3 Add any surface patterns to the cloak with a suitable tool. Decorate the crown to give the impression of jewels and cut crenelations into its rim.

Chess set

A chess set does not have to be black and white, as long as one set is glazed in a lighter colour than the other. The surface quality of the chosen glaze is important, because a high gloss may detract from the decoration of the pieces.

Fantasy castle

1 Centre 3.5kg (7lbs) of clay and throw a tall, tapering cylinder. The taller the cylinder is, the more impressive the end result will be. Compress the sides of the cylinder with a throwing rib to strengthen and shape the walls. Trim off any unevenness at the top of the cylinder.

A castle is traditionally associated with mystery and suspense; its silhouette alone can sometimes be enough to conjure up a sense of impending romantic adventure. The success of this project relies on the creative arrangement of its component cylinders. If the castle is to be lit up from within, the greater the number of turrets, the greater the visual impact will be.

2 Throw an identical second cylinder, and then a series of cylinders of varying sizes from which to make the turrets. Throw a squat, tapered cylinder with a base that measures twice the width of the first two cylinders. Leave them aside to stiffen. ▷

3 To make the roofs of the castle, stack-throw a series of varying conical forms. These cones will be stuck to the different cylinders at irregular angles to give the castle a romantic feel. Centre 0.3–0.7kg (³/₄– 1¹/₂lbs) of clay and begin to raise a V-shaped cone. △

4 Trim it away at its base to emphasize its point and slice it from the stack of clay. Repeat this process until you have thrown several slightly different forms. Leave them at one side to stiffen slightly. ▽

5 Once the large cylinders have stiffened but are still pliable, remove some of their base thickness with a knife. Alternatively, you can turn the forms in the usual way. △

6 With a sharp knife, slice vertically through one side of the walls of both cylinders. Open each cylinder out, easing the opening gradually wider. ▷

7 Gently bend the walls inwards until the cylinders look like two curved "W"s. Stand the two opened shapes next to each other and level off any difference in height.

8 Pare away the clay at an angle from the cut surfaces of the two forms, so that they fit together snugly when joined. Score the surfaces to be joined, apply slurry and press the pieces together. Smooth the joins firmly. Attach a coil of clay to the outside of each join and smooth it into place.

Assembling the pieces

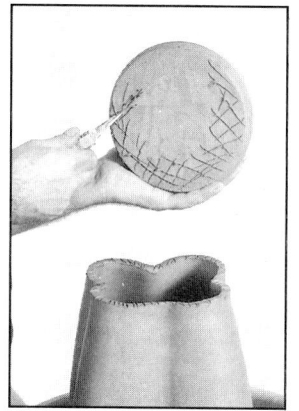

1 Score the top of the castle base and apply slurry. Take the short tapered cylinder and carefully score its base. Join this cylinder to the top of the castle base. ▷

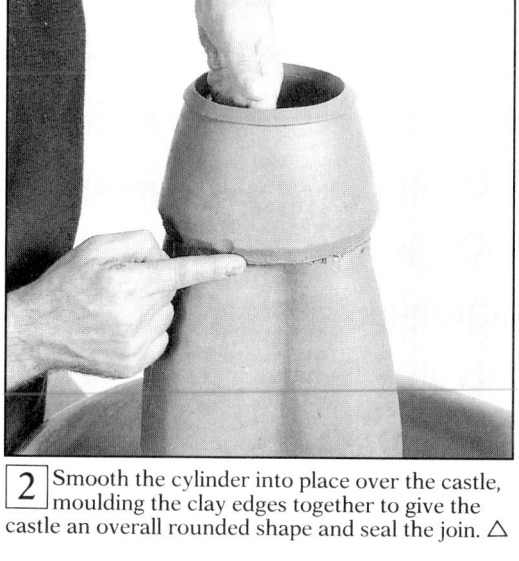

2 Smooth the cylinder into place over the castle, moulding the clay edges together to give the castle an overall rounded shape and seal the join. △

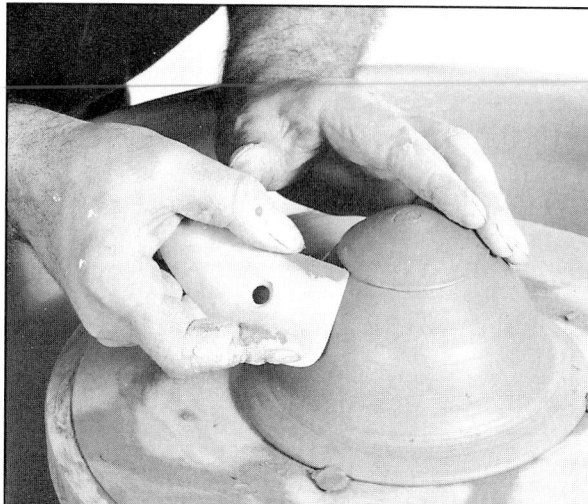

3 Centre a large roof cone and trim away the clay from its peak to make it rounded and more dome-like in shape. With a throwing rib, impress a cuff into the top of the roof for an additional decorative touch. △

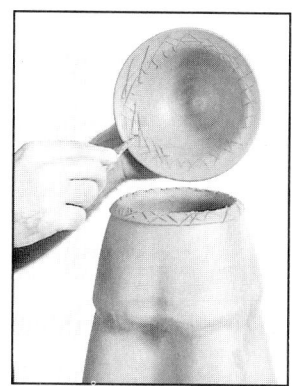

4 Attach it to the castle having scored the adjacent surfaces and applied slurry. Be careful not to distort the shape of the roof as you fix it in place.

5 Cut out a side section from one of the small cylinders so that it will sit in against the side of the castle shape. Roughly mark out the area on the castle to which this small tower is to be attached and score the surface of the clay. Apply slurry and press the tower into place.

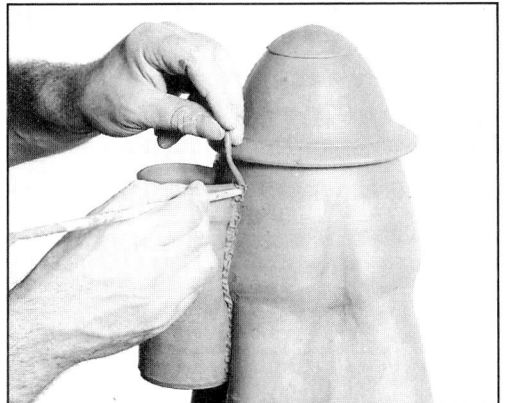

7 Pinch the top of a small roof cone, similar in diameter to the little tower. Cut out a curve in its wall so that it will fit neatly against the side of the castle. Score the surfaces to be joined, apply slurry and press the roof into place. Arrange a series of these small towers around the walls of the castle at different heights. You can mould them in any way you wish while they are still wet to create the castle design you have in mind.

6 Smooth the join carefully, reinforcing it with a coil of clay. Press the coil into place neatly using a wooden tool. Smooth the form off with a damp sponge. △

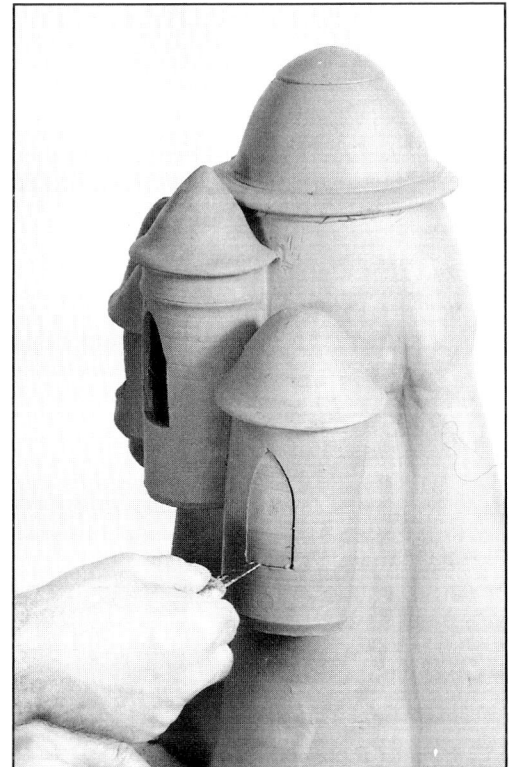

9 To decorate the roofs, roll out a sheet of clay and cut it up into little squares. Score the roofs, apply slurry and attach rows of these squares to give the effect of uneven tiles. Begin at the lower edge of the roof, smoothing the upper edge of each row before beginning the next. △

10 Leave the uppermost part of each roof bare and complete the layers of "tiles" with a thin coil of clay. Smooth this coil into the surface of the exposed roof. You can add as much detail as you want to the basic castle shape, adding more turrets until you feel happy with the silhouette you have created.

8 Cut out little windows in the walls of all the towers and corresponding holes in the wall of the castle behind these windows to allow the light through from within the castle. △

The finishing touches

1 To make the entrance to the castle, mark out an arched area midway up the side of the castle. Draw a zigzag line about a third of the way down from the upper curve and etch vertical lines down the top section to give the impression of a portcullis. Cut out the section of clay below the zigzag line with a knife and tidy the edge with a needle. Cut out several small blocks of flattened clay to make window ledges. Score them and attach them with slurry to the wall of the castle below each window. Smooth the join well.

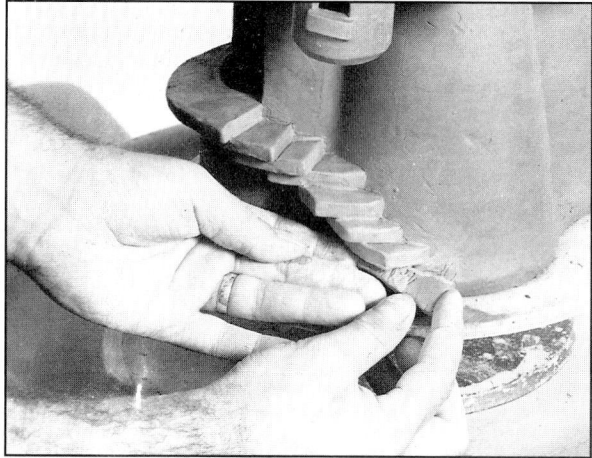

2 To make the winding staircase leading from the portcullis entrance, cut out a slightly triangular piece of flattened clay. Score the side of it and attach it with slurry to the wall of the castle below the entrance. Press it round following the curve of the wall. Attach several flat blocks of clay beneath this main step, overlapping each one in an irregular fashion, both to provide support and give the impression of a romantically worn stairway. △

3 You can wind the staircase around the wall of the castle as far as you wish. Trim around the base with a sharp knife to improve the finish of the castle and smooth the whole shape off.

Fantasy castle

The castle was glazed with a matt white glaze and then
sprayed with iron oxide. The roof tiles were wiped clean and
brushed with iron oxide alone, for a contrast in both colour
and texture between the roof, the steps, and the walls.

Index

Acknowledgments

The author and publisher would like to thank the
following people and organizations for their kind help
in the production of this book:

Potterycrafts Ltd., Campbell Road, Stoke-on-Trent,
for their generosity in supplying the wheel, the tools
and the clay for use in the book, and especially Ken
Shelton, their Marketing Manager, for his assistance:
Mr. A.V. Evershed (Principal) and Mr. R.A. Clarke
(Head of Department) of Milton Keynes College:
Craftsmen Potters Association for the loan of the
tools for the front cover photograph; Bruton
Photography, 22, Bruton Street, London W1X 7DA.